GENDER CINEMA AND SOCIETY

GENDER, CINEMA AND SOCIETY

Pooja Rai

HOW ACADEMICS
an imprint of Highlyy Publishing LLP

ISBN: 978-93-6009-573-4
First Published : 2025

Published by : HOW ACADEMICS
an imprint of Highlyy Publishing LLP

Correspondence Address :
4/30 A II Floor, Double Storey Buildings
Vijay Nagar, Delhi-110009
Editorial: +91 9811026449
Sales : +91 9999953412
Email: info@howacademics.com
Website: www.howacademics.com

Contents

Preface

The present study is an effort to investigate the relationship of Indian cinema and gender subordination with cultural hegemony. This study is based on primary data to find out the actual picture of Indian society through the respondents response about specific question related to cultural reproduction and gender subordination. This study is an inquiry of what kind of role of media in general and Indian cinema (Bollywood, Mainstream Cinema) in particular.

Indian Cinema has drawn inspiration from the styles and aesthetics of a great variety of cultural forms that have followed one upon another in India over the centuries, forming the vast cultural heritage. In the contemporary period, cinema has become one of the major parts of the human life; it plays an important role in entertainment, education and communication. Indian Cinema shows the reflection of different issues that are prevailing in the Indian society. This thesis will emphasis on Indian cinema which helps make Indian cinema extremely popular or unique and plays vital part in the Indian cinema which is dominated by and sustained with the help of such cinema.

The manner in which gender role or sexuality are constructed in cinema has a strong association to cultural and traditional factors. Culture (including tradition) must, however, be understood in its ancient and mythical contexts and their behavioural roots in society. These cultural elements help in understanding the nature of the construction of gender and sexuality in Indian Cinema. Various scholars make reference to Indian films as cultural products, signifying the important role that culture plays in the construction of characters (Gopalan, 1997; Dudrah, 2006). It seems that sexuality is structured and hegemonized through Culture, norms and traditions. Cultural Hegemony and gender subordination as a practice in our society is well stated; and how cinemas in India use the constructed gender identity as a tool to reinforce or challenge the status-quo (the notion of normality and the notion of difference). Cinema is the reflection of various things about social reality and raises questions of difference and sameness and how people understand their place within the conditions produced by Society or Cinema.

This study is an effort to explore the ways in which Indian cinemas have articulated the idea of the audience and also affected by the ideas of audience, and presents the argument that an Indian cinema must be necessarily multi-faceted in nature.

In recent years Indian cinema has revealed a lot, by not merely being a medium of mere entertainment but experimenting to highlight social and ethical cinema, which has a greater influence on the masses. The film fraternity slowly but gradually supports social matters and stands ready to take the trouble to build public visibility. However, a significant percentage of the filmmakers do follow the conventional formulation of film production that can have negative implications for the viewer.

The central role of cinema in culture in the conclusion is the provision of entertainment, schooling and teaching of moral values. It can create nationally desirable ideas and themes which contribute to a country's healthy development. It should strive to represent social problems (but not economically feasible for them), which will finally contribute to social cohesion in order to reinforce pro-social actions. Furthermore, it is often important to verify unwelcome, unsafe and hazardous concepts. Films can empower, encourage, and even change the beliefs a little differently.

There are many forms of behaviour, from the acts of children to the performance of their social roles, which seem to be absorbed from cinema around the world. Today, the extent to which cinema can affect its audience's minds is a contentious question. There are two think tanks on the subject. One school feels that movies typically have a brief impact and do not drastically alter the fundamental mindset of the viewer. The other school feels the effect is irreversible and provocative. The degree to which films bring about a shift in the mindset of the viewer and the degree to which blame can be fixed on the movie industry would be relevant to investigate. This is because the film does not have the same effect on all viewers as any person feels and acts. Similarly, the violent and vulgarity of all movies produced cannot be taken for granted. And if this is true on a general basis, the entire public cannot be radically affected because of their particular preferences, since people in this world vary.

The film is often regarded as a means of understanding the character, his / her social status and his / her community's values, including a folk tale, classic theatre, popular history and mediaeval morality. This is also a mechanism by which the entity reflects on a world of events that seem haphazard and unpredictable. Practical awareness is a precondition for the order. The necessity has emotional elements because the absence of explicit information creates fear within the person whose help he needs.

Since 1947, Indian cinema has greatly changed. It is known for its technique, and it has made a name for itself. Indian films contend with Western productions on the world level. Indian films have won coveted international awards and the rich cultural traditions of Indian dance and music today have a global audience due to the popularity of Indian cinema all over the world.

Culture is the overarching society's present, and the film represents a culture in particular. It reflects many trends, contemporary virtues, social fighting and living patterns. The essence of Indian society is depicted in Indian cinema. The linguistic diversity and, above all, the unity of the different cultural and religious religions, illustrates the racial and traditional ideals of Indian culture. Cultural interaction and dissemination, although obviously of an apolitical kind, were contentious given the hegemonic status of India in the region. It is important to get to know, perceive, and critique the concepts and signals from cradle to graves in a media and market culture. The media are a deep, frequently misunderstood source of cultural pedagogy: They tell us how to do, what to say, what to feel, what to believe, fear and what to do, etc. The media are instructional forms that tell us how to be men and women. We see how we wear, look and consume; how we respond to the members of various social groups; how we are famous, effective, and prevent failure; how we comply with the prevalent set of expectations, principles, traditions and institutions. Accordingly, acquiring vital media literacy is an essential opportunity for people and individuals to learn how to deal with a seductive cultural environment. The learning about how socio-cultural exploitation can read, critique and resist can motivate you against dominant media and culture types. It will strengthen the autonomy of citizens over media culture and provide people with more control over their cultural climate.

Despite all rules, traditionally speaking, women continue to be perceived as frail and secondary to men. It is particularly interesting because in movies all these forms of injustice are expressed.

Such kind of study definitely brings some hope in the arena of research to engagement of scholars in such topics to concentrate and explore further reality to create alternative of inequality, injustice, exclusion, hegemony, subordination, subaltern and so on.

Chapter 1
Introduction

Introduction

In recent years, Indian Cinema has shown much by trying to display the social and responsible cinema with a stronger effect on the public, and by not contained in pure entertainment. Film fraternity gradually but steadily supports social problems and is prepared to take the pride in raising public consciousness. A significant number of filmmakers also adopt the conventional definition of film making, which can influence the audience.

Indian cinema is one of the most important and strong instruments to deal with complex social issues by way of a screenplay. Films have been a vital medium since they were founded in 1913 for communicating social insights and conditions and for them to continue to act as an important entertainment mode for the masses (Gupta and Gupta, 2013). It is also very fascinating to comprehend whether films shape society or not (Bhugra, 2006). It is very difficult to understand. Indian cinema experiments with different genres in order to create a successful formulation, which works well with the audience and takes a lead on mythology, comedy, and horror.

In the 60 years since Independence, Indian films have undergone numerous Changes, including a transition to the remakes of "Bollywood", successful Hollywood movies, from classical mythological blockbusters. The popularity of individual cinemas in the Indian film industry also played an important role for women. But they changed their position overnight, from being quite autonomous to telling the story. Before referring to changes, it is important to understand the importance of Indian cinema today in the world. Surveys and studies show that nearly four billion people are watching Indian films in over 100 countries worldwide. The Indian film industry has been recognized as the world's largest industry with more than 1000 films released in over 20 languages per year and less than 400 films made annually in Hollywood based on records available. In India, approximately 3.3 billion tickets are sold every year, with the highest number of theater entries. A further statistical series states that around 750 films were filmed in 72 studios each year and showed to almost 70 million weekly audiences in approx. 12,000 cinemas; Lata Mangeshkar is the world's most recorded Guinness Book artist, some unusual records, and in a thousand films Helen has danced.

Ninety percent of its sales on the Indian market are derived from non-English films, primarily films from Hindi and South India and other movies in the region. The industry projected growth from USD 3.2 billion to USD 5 billion by 2014 is CRISIL Research (2010). Since industry in Bollywood plays an important role, trends in business and society have changed drastically from the past to the present.

Bollywood, part of Mumbai Indian film industry, can be called the domestic film industry, as they produce Hindi-language movies with the most watched screens. Mumbai was the world's largest movie center, but Madras & Calcutta compete vigorously in India. The film industry of Bollywood was called Hollywood by the US film industry. It's one of the most innovative, important industries and surprises, given the fact that half of the movie theaters are in South India.

Then there is a question: why was Mumbai so famous as a center? Mumbai was the center of the film industry of India. It had a modern harbor, town with European influences and claims that were minute to the history and society of Native America. Moreover, the main Hindu-Muslim struggles were hostile against religious beliefs in South Asia. In relatively harmonious Mumbai, both races and religions existed. English drama and poetry were thriving in Mumbai. Several Western ideas, stimulated by the English, were summed up with Indian ideas. Throughout the past three thousand years, ghosts, avatars, gods and spirits from Indian mythology have been combined with modern American, Marx and theories and symbols.

In the course of the struggle for freedom, cinema was used as a tool for illustrating the anger and the opinions of the nationalist and the British colonial leaders. Yet film became a medium to deal with social problems and issues following independence. Bollywood represented a community desired and feasible by films.

Indian cinema produces between 800 and 1000 films each year, twice as many as Hollywood (Sridehar and Mattoo, 1997). The world's largest producer of feature films is Indian. "Bollywood" with its headquarters in Bombay, now Mumbai, is a big part of the Indian movie industry, focuses on Hindi films. Furthermore, films are produced in local languages such as Bhojpuri, Bengali and Tamil, to name a few. These films end up being successful locally but block the audiences across boundaries throughout the country due to language barrier. In view of diversity, films are the most powerful way of understanding the social standards, perceptions and cultural variants and actions of the audience and of transmitting them to them. In the reflection of society films play a dual role, but are at the same time important for the shaping and influence of culture. Since the start of the Indian cinema industry, the film brotherhood has tried to transmit social messages by experimenting in several genres. Sometimes these attempts fail, while others have called on the public to make the box office new heights.

Founded in 1913, "Raja Harish Chandra" (Pillania 2008) has become the dominance and the most powerful means of communication in the country. Movie was a silent mythological image, paving the way for the filmmakers of the day (Verma, 2019). The films then represented Indian deep and rich heritage by portraying the great epics of Indian history-Ramayana and Mahabharata. Indian films published their first talkie in 1931, Alam Ara, who paved the way for Indian film's future. The industry then began to experiment with animation and color films. Different genres such as comedy, romance, action and thriller were also emerging in this period.

Social issues such as farmer pain and untouchability were highlighted during cinematic exposure in the 1930s, around the time of economic and social reform in India, and the fight to free themes of movies like Mehboob Khan's Mother India (1957) and Bimal Roy's Do Bhiga Zameen (1953) (Murthy C.S.H.N, 2011). Although parallel but distinctive from stereotypes, this alternative form of film has taken a deeper look into socially conscious and politically placed matters with support for the form of public funding of cinema since 1970.

This taste for Indian movies started to create new waves for filmmakers who were able to go beyond music and entertainment and who had the opportunity to bring a social cause to the world. Bollywood films have to be investigated in establishing their identity in the Indian Diaspora because of their growing success in electronic media and Hindi films.

But the alternative movement was unfortunately unable to move for a long time and, due to two main reasons, the first, although somehow monetarily supported by the government, was beginning to fade out in the 1990s, however, certain financial or political constraints were present at that time, there were restricting film production. The government's fiscal support began to decline, since the movie buffs wanted to see more since the movies lacked the entertainment or, so to say, the X- factor. This led various next-generation filmmakers to pursue creative ways of expressing the social message. One format that was successful was for entertainment to be combined with social communication attributed to the success of films such as 3 Idiots, Munnabhai MBBS, Taare Zameen Par, etc.

Cinema has been one of the major influences in our modern life, and also is art, photography, architecture, literature, playing, painting, and music. "These four have a major role in today's world, mixing technology, entertainment and esthetics and are often seen in the various types of film (photograph taken and filmed in a celluloid camera), film is business and entertainment". Cinematography is esthetics. A movie, common or parallel, is a visual story art that represents the contemporary society in which its dunces, with rich inputs of music, storyline, cast and script. Film derives its substance, ideas and imaginations from emotional drama, candy floss romance, and action thrillers. The picture films create surreal or intrusive waves of deception, they must be in harmony with society's aspirations and the fundamental urge of humankind to recreate and enjoy. For a century, film has been a tabu and an utter no-no-no-life on its long journey. Social dynamics have always controlled cinema's contents. Every film's main protagonist struggles against villagers who demonstrate contemporaneous evil - from local moneylenders to country hawks to advocates of dowries, donations and modern terrorists. It provides an economic, political, technological and economic growth platform. Films are helpful in the knowledge of ancient world history. Many countries around the world are interested in filmmaking through their own industry; Hollywood, which enjoys the entire world and does not only shocks the world with the advances in technology, is amongst the most powerful, coordinated, famous and influential. A film is not just a visual treat for his or her audience; it also represents the societal, economic and political environment in which a person lives.

Influence on Society

Indian film has greatly influenced Indian culture, but looking back at Indian society, Bollywood has also influenced and transformed it as it evolves dramatically from a soft movie period into a contemporary scenario. Maybe Bollywood has profoundly affected the nationalism of India, as regional film even becomes a part of the narrative of Incredible India. Cinema is the strongest platform for the most vibrant way possible to decide your own plot. It is the strongest means of speech and a source of entertainment for all age groups. We have seen earlier in the wars how Indian movements motivated Indians, through their songs, to fight and achieve patriotism among peoples and national integration as part of global power.

In India, the legacy of their past generations has been borne, as they all believed in the arranged marriage tradition and practices it. Yet again, Bollywood drama has helped to show us more holistically the nature of different partnerships. The community has also been helped by numerous films, which have seen successful marriages between castes in India. Film has played a significant role in expressing our romantic and violent feelings with us. Our spirit is the songs of these movies. Even there is a hip-hop or a Bollywood tadka song in every party, festival or wedding. It is the music that follows them in moments of joy or sorrow as we speak about the teens in our culture. In sleepless nights, it also supports them.

India's films have a very positive and lasting effect on the mind, while the tender minds of the audience have very serious impact on cheap and shabby films. It is generally felt that today's crimes are all due to cinema effects. Apart from accessible and demonstrative subjects, the communications are tarnished. Our culture and society are being spoiled. The mental health of young people is badly affected by cinema and television. They fail to devote more time with studies and athletic sports. Children in schools and culture do not have positive results and are affected by the negative aspect of Indian cinema.

This reason is not to so easily dismiss cinema or TV. Specific and selective programs are the desirable act. The students will have to watch films with strong social message. The TV show films should be limited and for a fixed period. The film influences people's minds greatly. It has a high educational value. In the field of education expansion, it can achieve wonderful results. Some subjects, including science and geography, may be learned more easily with the aid of conversations. Students and the public can also be taught in a very efficient way by means of movies in the form of road senses, rules of hygiene and civic sense. In various countries many successful experiments on the use of films as a means of education have been carried out. Feature films for school and university students have been made, and students profit from them.

Our society's youngest generation is the one that is adversely affected by the changes that have occurred in our society, whether motivated or depressed. Indian cinema is highly sensitive to the presentation of stories based entirely on malicious acts against women such as sexual harassment, rape or killing. These films have been made with the aim of raising the awareness of these vulgar acts and making them aware of the effects. These films are not produced to create a big blast at the box office, but to convey a social message among people. The performers in these films are courageous, as they are faced with a lot of media attention as they have presented this critical topic to the audience. Since the film, Talwar was very open to the public in real life. The actors in the film faced several newspapers and the media as to why they have been struggling with this controversial subject.

Since the most of the Indian citizens are of the middle class and the lower class, their families are the most important things. This is portrayed in a film named Drishyam by Ajay Devgan, where he has a small middle-class family and his daughter was harassed during a nature camp by a police general's son and in turn of events the daughter and the wife murdered the son and told Ajay about it. He then decides to save his family by concealing the dead body. As he loves to watch films and he takes idea of what other actors had done in similar films and use those tricks for his real life from incidents from different films. He saves his family activities at the end, because it was a crime he did. This demonstrates that a coin has two sides and that everything has its own advantages and disadvantages. Nobody is good at over-exceeding something. Films have had both optimistic and harmful consequences for Indian culture.

Cinema films can influence people's thinking. Society and social trends have been changed by Introduction of cinema. In society, they have introduced new modes. They can directly influence our personal life. However, it is also a force which has the potential to control society. There is therefore immense damage in our society if a film depicts scenes of moral degradation or violates our moral standards. We know that many young people have been misled by indecent images, filthy, intolerant and crime images that can very easily fascinate impressive youngsters. Film also has an excellent power to make people believe in what they see on the screen. It is not just a matter of course.

Cinema can directly influence our social life. Films could go a long way towards the awakening of national consciousness. Through a skilled adaptation of morally, socially and educationally good subjects and the introduction to popular sentiment, films could also, in large measure, form and guide public opinion.

In films, the different traditions of the country in different areas help the society learn and learn more about them, because not everybody can visit every part, but the films give a better idea of human activities and thus we understand them better. We are able to understand these traditions and customs throughout different places of the country.

Our films first projected anecdotes from the Silent Cinema era, ancient Indian themes glorifying, resurrecting in the memories of the people, the glorious past and tradition of the Hindu mythology.

When Indian movies began to represent modern Indian life, social films came into existence as opposed to mythological films or folklore. Although many of these films deal with the tales between boys and girls or the drama of the perennial war between mother-in-law and daughter-in-law, they were daring in calling orthodoxies into question and inducing change. After the Sarada Act was passed in 1929, the Indian family – the adult unmarried daughter was introduced to as a new member. This was a significant turning point of social change. Indian films have contributed in their own way to this revolutionary change. While most films were escapist entertainment, they subliminally rendered a commitment to social progress without a deliberate social statement.

Filmmakers evaded overt racist messages, owing to tight political repression, but also inadvertently and implicitly exposed their tendency. Some filmmakers have displayed portraits of Gandhi, Nehru, Rajaji or Netaji and occasionally Karl Marx, hanging in hero's living spaces, showed their affiliation with the national struggles.

Often the meaning of the struggle for independence had also been embedded in myths, historical and mythological films. In the 'Amar Raj' by J.B.H. Wadia, for example, the hero retrenched a tyrannical ruler and proclaimed "democracy" who could have taken over the throne. Sohrab Modi's 'Sikandar', with the Sohrab Modi and Prithviraj Kapoor, on the invasion of India by Alexander evoked strong nationalist feelings. The Gandhian principles for the elimination of "untouchable" were transmitted by Prabhat's dedication, biographical film on the Martyr, "Eknath". The British censors objected to "Mahatma", this is the original title of the film, and it had to be transformed into "Dharmatma" by the distributors.

If the Bollywood films were to illustrate individuality and the relation between person and society, it would be an interesting research. Obviously, like all other forms of art, films also show the proper nature and position of the society at that time, but certain forms of art not only represent the present situation in the society, but also provide a new trend to lead and practical society which make these films a masterpiece. It is considered, according to the artist as a careful re-creation of the reality. Of course, the object of this selective recreation is not to show the events as they are, because Aristotle claims that philosophic literature is of greater metaphysical importance than fact, since "history portrays things like they are and fiction describes them as they can and need to be".

The sweep of globalization in India and the fast expanding consumerism change the face of commercial cinema in India, resulting in socio-economic changes. In the 1970s, film tastes and presentations were greatly affected by producers and the audience, but now financial "market forces" become more important. Diasporic tastes, their nostalgic perspectives of Indian-ness and the differences in the tastes of urban audiences in urban areas and produce new kinds of commercial films in comparison to rural viewers. We are yet to see how Indian film keeps affluent, marginal and low- medium-income audiences isolated from their traditional tastes. In Indian cinema previously untouchable subjects surfaced and even got censored in India. Films, the most undeniably powerful media in art, are the principal influence in transformation in culture and reinforce the ideals of autonomy because they want to present things, circumstances and individuals as they should be.

Film directors shape a movie that can modify the view of people in the future. From the outset, Indian film has produced some of the best actors, the rarest and most exceptionally creative, in its glorious past of more than 100 years.

Portrayal of women in Indian Cinema

Films mirror culture. We get to know the society at the time when we see films from a particular time. Films also play an important role in social change. Films spread the spirit of nationalism among common people during the Indian war for independence. Films underwent many changes, with changing times. But the development in Indian cinema's portrayal of women has not yet captured our society's progress. As film lovers are greater than the rest of the world in India, the effect of films on Indian society is immense. The Indian film industry is still a patriarchal society. Even if times change, men's ideals and dreams still occupy the majority of Indian cinema's space. Some of this is regressive and infringing on women. And the number of films with important roles for women is growing. And it is true. So, it is important to think about how far we are going and what problems need to be tackled in Indian cinema's representation of women.

The first Indian film in which women's actors are in the leading role is Mother India (1957). Until the 1980s, leading actresses played important roles. Films had magnificent stories at that time that totally reflected society. But filmmakers used to add 'vamp' characters in the films to provide musical entertainment with sexually explicit or degrading results. Even now, that culture has not changed. Manufacturers incorporate products to gain market success. Since the 1980s it was just a hero-centric film that began to play the role of leading actress. This pattern is observed by most commercial films. Many leading actresses have played important roles recently. As more female directors, writers, actors, etc. enter in the film industry, the condition of the representation of female characters increases.

Most mainstream films are centered on men. In these films, lead actresses are treated like glam dolls. In many films of today, women are sexualized without need. In addition, in the name of item songs, incorporating pornographic lyrics and dances is particularly disrespectful to women and adversely affects young people.

Item songs such as shown in Figure 1.1 show people that it's all right for women to be teased. It's all right to look at them voyeuristically. According to the first ever UN global study (2014) sponsored by the UN of women in popular films around the world, the Indian film industry toped in objectification to women. Leading actors are displayed as saviors always. Women are demonstrated to be either helpless or crafty villagers. Generally speaking, hero is the one who solves all the heroin problems included. Films portray actresses as unreally gorgeous. Therefore, not only the female audience but also the actresses have a lot of trauma and insecurity. Stalking and teasing in Indian films are portrayed as love. Women are in love with these abusers in many mainstream movies. Because of that, in the name of love, several young men harass women. In 2015, an Indian man was accused of stalking in Australia, and the court ruled after an investigation of the incidents that his fascination with Bollywood-based films was the cause of his behaviour.

For the better, times are changing. As more women as directors, producers, actresses etc. join the movie industry, we witness strong female characters in films. The picture of "good girl" was forced into female earlier lead roles. Heroines have been portrayed as submissive, are more likely to be home-built, not career-oriented, and silently bear the brunt of abusive men. The women in movies are now more realistic and many actresses do not play such meaningless roles.

Figure 1.1: Item songs from Bollywood (https://www.google.com/search?sxsrf=ALeKk02p9JSbLkSJNQJ6NYf3Fhmz7yNbuA: 1612886295641)

From the 1950s this time, the problem of poverty was tackled. That, though rural, had rich and diverse traditions. Many films from Bollywood golden age are so well known that they recall the future generation. This was also the period when women played a significant part in films and had a lot to do with the promotion of the films. In Hindu films, women and the masculine actors were given an equally dominant role. Mother India made by Mehboob in 1957 was just a few examples. Ten years after the independence of India from the British rule, the film was made.

Such instance is the 1989 film, directed by Ketan Mehta, Mirch Masala, which shows women in Indian film this changing role. A story about Sonbai (Smita Patile) in the West part of pre-independence India employed in a chili factory. Her husband gets a job in the train and goes to town. Meanwhile, Naseeruddin Shah's subedar (or tax collector) arrives for tax collection and is attracted to Sonbai. He asked the headman of the village, Mukhi, to take him, but the headman brought the wrong woman. The next day Sonbai passed the camp of Subedar and was stopped by the Subedar and captured. She liberates herself and rushes to her work in the chili factory. A forgery is provided by an old Muslim watcher, Abu Miyan (Om Puri). Mukhi's aunt, the Mukhiain is a parallel track that her husband does not treat well. After discovering that the village males and her own husband are allied with the Subedar to hand it over to Sonbai, she is attempting to obtain help for Sonbai. The people rudely smash Mukhiain's protest, and Subedar, accompanied by all the men of the village, reaches a factory that smashes the watchman at the factory doors. In the final scene, when other women in the plant unexpectedly throw chili powder bags on their faces the Subedar approaches Sonbai.

Mirch Masala's example does not mean the females have always been left behind in movies. A more dominant image of women is also represented in several films. The body has been an essential part of the success of an actress in the recent history of cinema. They talk about the time spent in the gym. Sri Devi, who leads the 1980s, is nicknamed 'thunder thighs', for instance. Sri Devi spends hours in a maquila bed, just like other female stars, portraying the violent and dominant character. She dances and struggle the men out in Himmatwala, a previous film. She handled and defeated the villagers herself. In some films her role needs to be balanced with two or three male stars. In Joshila (1989), when cast against her, two of the top male heroes in the film would hardly hold their role alone. This shows that by this time women's attitude and perception had completely changed.

Further changes were made later in the 1990s by the Hindi cinema. Various films at that time showed women's changing role in Indian film. The first were Mohra, Mr. Roma Singh, Mr. Kumar, Raveena Tandon, Mr. Shetty, Mr. Naseeruddin and Mr. Jindal. They were also produced with Akshay Kumar (like Amar Saxena) in 1994.

Their presence made the story no difference. The more globalized India becomes, the more backward Bollywood films. Some of the hit films from the 1990s after liberalization, revealed that the women retained their homes and men received the bread for a conventional way of living. As Madhuri Dixit stole her hearts on the Hum Aapke Hain Kaun, one of the biggest hits of the nineties, she also found a heroine trend that never would put herself before her family's desires and desires. Women were back in trend in their caring role as homemakers. Hai Kaun also established a heroine trend that never would make its own dreams better than their family's aspirations and wishes. The careful role of women in the household was revisited.

The most recent movies in the late 1990's such as 'Kabhi Khushi Kabhi Gum' 'Kuch Kuch Hota Hai', 'Dil Toh Pagal Hai', 'Biwi No.1.' None of the movies created as women portrayed career women by contemporary young filmmakers. But the women that had failed in their love life showed themselves to take a career. Karisma is loses dancer for Madhuri Dixit in Dil Toh Pagal Hai whose main purpose in life is to meet her life partner. Sushmita Sen was shown as a 'Biwi No.1' role model, but she was also a home breaker, and Karisma Kapoor's forgiving housewife in the same movie 'wins' her man back.

She also took on the traditional role of his wife, the Dil Chahta Hai film, which was a film of the X generation, produced by a young producer. While the three men in the movie had identities other than their romantic, the women had no identity for themselves. Only one character (Dimple Kapadia), who has a career but does not end happily, finds a regular girlfriend as the guy who loves her (Akshay Khanna).

Many of the film directors have trained abroad and are inspired by western ideals in their way of life. Hollywood films have been watched but through the female characters in their films they have returned to traditional Indian ideals and conservative ideals.

A definite distinction between the heroine and vamp, the good and the bad girl will be seen in this way. The vamp drank, was still born and her bad acts were punished. Like a "foreign", a smoker and a spoilt-brother, Saira Bano was shown in the Purab Pachim of Manoj Kumar and taught by the hero. The good ones still appear as beautiful ladies. In separate avatars with a change of name and position only was the image of an ideal daughter or wife or girl-in-law used. Singh (2007) shows that modern film has gained a great deal of its appeal from Indian mythology. This shares primarily male prejudice's desires and importance and dramatizes female sexual fantasies. Therefore, a woman is depicted as either an angel or a demon.

The cinema represents political philosophies, social ideals, group behaviour, speeches and clothing in society and also represents on culture. Furthermore, the movie stars have stepped into politics from their imagination to become powerful figures who lead the destiny of millions. This includes a number of women actresses who served as the custodian of society. This growth demonstrates that the female aspect has become known not only in movies but also in the real world. Throughout Indian cinema, the role played by women serves as a model for other women with less chance to pursue. As Indian cinema is a huge success, Indian women in the movies can easily relate to these female characters. With Indian cinema. The cinema can therefore be viewed as a genuine symbol of society, and this perception contributes to a better understanding of society.

Gender and Sexuality in Indian Culture

Women make up about half of the human society's workforce. They have been making the same contribution to the development and maintenance of human society from the advent of human society on earth by the means of reproduction, socialization and the administration of household workers. However, notwithstanding that the role played by women is often characterized as subservient to men by women themselves. Moreover, almost all of the world's religious scriptures grant men and women unequal status. Maybe that these religious scriptures have two distinct facets. Woman means a biological person as a gender category whose composition and characteristics differ from a man.

Figure 1.2: Gender subordination in Indian movie Aandhiyan (https://en.wikipedia.org/wiki/Aandhiyan)

In the category of sex, a woman is a social being who is supposed to act in a certain way from the social and cultural standpoints which makes her appear less than men. In other words, they are just characterized by their organic reproductive attributes as a sex category. This distinguishing is rendered socially by the definition of their positions according to socio-cultural principles. As their body is anatomically different from men who are considered more muscular and taller, they are considered belonging to the weaker sex as shown in Figure 1.2, Figure 1.3 and Figure 1.4.

Figure 1.3: Gender subordination in Indian movie (https://thewire.in/culture/the- toxic-masculinity-of-salman-khan)

Among the people of our society, there are many reasons for this kind of process of thinking. Women are considered to be the most vulnerable among the various marginalized sectors of society. They are subject to some drawbacks, such as being marginalized economically and socially. Sharing the gender related inequality and subordination.

Figure 1.4: Gender subordination in Indian movie Mujhse Shaadi Karogi (https://en.wikipedia.org/wiki/Mujhse_Shaadi_Karogi)

Women are denied access to power and socio-economic status which is generally given to men. Women alone are expected to assume responsibility for household work. No matter how major a female succeeds in athletics, business, science and technology or business, society always expects a woman to be responsible for carrying out all household duties because of her gender. The socio-economic, cultural and religious influences establish a psychological perception regime that finds a woman more vulnerable than a man and that is why any part of society treats women as secondary.

In order to promote greater equality between men and women, various positive advances took place. The marriage age of girls from 15 to 18 is most significant, making it easier for them to enter higher education levels. People began to have nuclear households, so housewives wanted less time in reproductive and childcare practices than before.

Despite these progressive changes, certain lasting societal constraints do not convert these steps into real equality between women and men. The preference for male children is apparent in many cultural traditions. The main explanation for the persistent love over the centuries is the importance of many traditions and rituals among people for male children. The business institutions of our traditional society have enshrined questions about the lineage and ethnicity to such a degree that they affect the behaviour, like sex-selectorial abortion, to a greater or lesser extent.

The fact that women in India have accomplished tremendous success over the last 50 years is not disputed, but still in the male-dominated society they must battle a variety of challenges and social evils. The daughter and son share of the property was issued by the Hindu Code Bill. Women are no longer considered the property of men under the Marriage Act. Love is now called a personal situation and a wife who feels miserable is entitled to divorce. But one thing is the enactment of the statute and its incorporation into society's common thought is entirely different. In the Indian Constitution they must throw off the fetters of slavery and superstitions and show themselves true and their integrity and status. It should enable the government and community to eradicate dowry, analphabetism and ignorance. The problem of dowry in this country has taken on a dangerous shape. The girl's parents pay the brides men and their selfish fathers and mothers thousands and lakhs. If the Brides 'parents do not offer promised papers, the barbaric and jealous Brides' family members resort to afflicting torment of married women. In such situations, several women are killed. The dowry deaths of the barbaric and inhumane are absolutely horrendous and barbarous offences. The girls should be brave enough not to marry the boys who challenge their parents for their dowry. The children should also refuse to get married if their parents ask for their dowry. Unfortunately, though, there are very few boys of this kind and their conscience. And physicians, engineers, teachers and the officials do not hesitate to be sold to the affluent fathers of timid and shy girls.

It is possible to state that the concept behind the Hindu social organization is a closely-structured system in which property, women and traditional purity exist, based upon above mentioned facts of the role of women in Indian history. A few Brahms have introduced different practices and traditions, which speak about the preference of a male child and the supremacy of the male in our family and society. The principal religious reason for the preference of a son is the Hindu belief, which is more widespread among India's highest castes than that only a male child can provide the appropriate oblations for the soul of a deceased parent. Such convictions were also found in India among other religious groups, including the Sikhs and Muslims. In addition, in order to preserve male dominance in social and religious affairs, they have interpreted religious scriptures.

A tradition is born and resides on the firm basis of thoughts and values, which enriches or retains a tradition. The foundation for a custom is the social system and the sum of the circumstances that arise at the time. In order to create a comfortable tradition, the existing class often wishes to avoid compromising its interests. This tradition is related to the weak classes of society. All our religious, socioeconomic, literature and cultural practices so far have in effect been placed by a minority on a majority.

Gender and Sexuality in Indian Cinema

Relevant analyses of gender in Indian movies are not particularly based on male audiences of the genre who are assumed to have a largely masculine and patriarchal identity with a small number of discursive roles that are specified for them in films. These discursive positions are considered relatively homogeneous through the various films, including entire genres, not merely to be communications, but also to shape structures of meaning and thought expressed through the visual and other language which order experience and actions. It is important to understand the history and background of cinematic representation studies to learn how and why this movement takes place between assumptions about textual strategies that create meanings and public significance in the context of Hindi films. Many of the theoreticians writing in this area were concerned about the direct effects of the media on actions. Empirical analyses on gender equality strongly suggest that representations in the media are used by readers and viewers as 'models'.

The triangular transition to the strengthening of gender inequality from potentially "daunting" representations of women in the media to the negative transformation of the "self-image of women" takes place equally flatly. This doesn't only seem logical, but only common sense. The actual facts of existence, as are evidence of research into media representation for the majority of India's women, mainly rural and poor or urban and poor. Increasing sexual permission in the screen is clearly seen in the iconography-chain that binds and degrades women as another complicating factor. In this sense it fuses into individual heroines the conventional Hindi films dichotomy of vamp / prostitute / dancing girl and chaste wife and makes woman more appealing to some men only. Whereas, the psychological consistence of heroines is less. Male audiences would have had to cheer on the dance of girls before and then silence in respect of the heroine's loyal piety.

Function of subordinates (leading role defined for male leadership)

- Wife of the protagonist
- The wife of the main character
- Girlfriend / love interest of male actor
- Helps male actor to achieve its objective
- Less than the men's lead screen time
- Role of alternative position
- Dancing vamp / shortcuts
- Nightclub dancing / bar dancing / dancing cabaret.
- Call girl / prostitute.
- Parents in front of yourself
- Committees financial interests for the sake of the family at least once
- Willing to give the spouse / male leader a priority over his own interests
- Not rebellious to customs / social norms developed
- Family honor and social status surrender Sacrifices
- Orienting your career
- Home Maker: Children's treatment, in-law treatment
- Accommodation activities are carried out
- Lives in a family together
- No particular mention of the interests of her career

The origins of Indian film epics stem from the characterization of women for script and story. The two biggest and most celebrated epics of their history are the Ramayana, the story of Prince Rama, and Sita's aunt, and Mahabharata. In the Ramayana, Sita is the female protagonist who stands by her husband and cares throughout his difficulties. After Rama married Sita, Kaikeyi, Rama's founder, who is one of the queens of the kingdom and who wants to have her own son Bharath as her husband, the King Dasaratha, manipulated her husband into banishing the empire's eldest son, Rama. He agreed to be in exile for 14 years, and Rama, who told his dad that he was going to do anything to help his dad. His wife Sita leads him in exile to the woods with her husband.

Rama and Sita live in the woods together with one of the brothers of Lakshmana to protect the wise people of the devils who live in the trees. Throughout this time, Sita was captured by Ravana, a demon king who wants her to be his queen. Rama tries to kill Ravan to take back his beloved Sita. In the battle against demon king Ravana of Lanka Rama has made efforts to support him by making friends and forming ties with different people in the jungles. As Rama comes home to his parents, he must have asked Sita, his aunt, in some versions of the epic to go through and bath in fire as evidence that she was innocent. That's what Sita agrees.

The idea behind the fire bath is that Sita will prove to the world that she remained unstamped by Ravana during her time of prison and did not succeed in some kind of physical relationship or breach of Ravana. It's so pure, that the fire god, Agni, can't give her even a little burn. This is commonly known as Sita's purity test. Rama is the incarnation of Vishnu the Lord and Sita his wife, the incarnation of Lakshmi the Goddess, Lord Vishnu's wife, as mentioned in a Hindu religion. Sita's pureness lead into the Virgin Complex in society, in which the woman, child carrier, and linens enhancer is meant to be as clean as Sita in Ramayana. This is a strong concept in India's minds. Films and movie stories are based on the strong images epic characters create in people's minds several times.

"We have looked at stories that have taken the time to the test, like Ramayana, the Mahabharata ... this is proof of how powerful they are", said Pattanaik. This is because God tales, myths and epics are tales that people have been told in their lives. Its stories with which children are brought up. Since this is a major part of everyday life, they internalize the values of these stories to life. Pattanaik says that epics and stories are heard in their minds throughout their lives creating subjective realities which lead to their visions and perceptions on the world. The subjective truth is internalized. These world views then dominate their ideas, their attitudes, their beliefs and their approach to life situations including administration and business. The internalization of epics in movie history generates epic ideas and visions in people's minds that then go into the field of popular culture and affect character assumptions in the film.

The Indian cinema industry has been a popular source of entertainment since its inception in the 1930s and spans decades. Given the waves of theaters and blockbusters that have made it big, most of the films released share something-characters that adhere to a society's concept of masculinity are depicted by men and women's roles are reduced to misogynistic ideals. This led to questions about gender stereotypes, the quality of media viewed by the public and the misinterpretation of a balanced society, due to the absence of equal treatment both on the and off-screen.

Several films reinforce their opinions on the ideal woman often by supporting characters, they are playing love interests or enjoy professions that seem nourishing, emerging as weak and degrading entities with little time to reflect and argue. In addition to being a long way from reality, these films establish an impression of the potential and interests of women and so implicitly plant in people's minds the seeds of injustice.

In the Bollywood industry the evolution of women can be seen through the spectator's look. The perception of women by film enthusiasts and the like, influenced by factors such as policy, economic structure and culture, helped to establish borders on and behind the scenes. The English art critic and novelist, John Berger, Ways of Seeing said, "Women appear in men's act. In his 1972 essay on art criticism. Men are watching, women watch themselves being watched" (Berger, 2003) and applied the idea of the 'male view' to his study of women's portrayal in media. Within this context, it is not shocking that the Indian film industry is often regarded as a men- dominated world, considering the impossible ideals seen in various films and the lack of women in representation behind movies.

According to the Geena Davis Institute 2017 report, in Bollywood, only one in 10 directors are women. Other statistics show that the time of the screen for women is just 31.5% compared to 68.5% for male actors. In Bollywood we have shown the female figures through eyes from a largely masculine perspective, which leads to age- old stereotypes and gender distances in film due to the disparity in number of men compared to the women in main off-screen processes like writing, film-making and direction.

The cinema has become the most popular mode of entertainment as it is easily accessible. The Indian movie industry has a broad world view with around 3.6 billion people on large screens. The film industry is a global player. A part of their duty is to get rid of these misunderstandings and misinterpretation in a country in where actors step beyond their profession into heroes who are idiotic and caring.

The way Kabir Singh depicted a miserable relationship as a love form was examined and displayed the main lead played by Shaid Kapoor as a man-child who treats his lover like his property. Kabir Singh was one of his highest films in 2019. Kabir Singh is the emblem of toxic manhood, but is forgiven and eventually wins over his woman. The success of this nonapologetic glorification of misogyny in the box office shows how far it remains to be done.

However, the changes of time have shown many successes directed by women Zoya Akhtar's- Gully Boy, Fire and Earth's- Deepa Mehta, Gauri Shinde's popular film English Vinglish- some of the many works that gradually transform the industry by depicting women from all walks of life. Pink was an advanced and inspiring women's consent film. It included Tapsee Pannu and Amitabh Bachchan. Under My Burkha, directed by Alankrita Shrivastava, Lipstick Under My Burkha had several problems with the Central Film Certification Board which raised double standards for decisions of the film body, considering that films containing derogatory women's jokes are routinely adopted by this Board. Performing artists like Priyanka Chopra, Anushka Sharma and Kangana Ranaut are linked in the film with powerful women and create and support women's films with Queen & Vidya Balan and Kahaani.

Although great progress has recently been made to represent women of different lifestyles, other warnings accompany them. Project Mangal illustrated ISRO's women scientists hard work and contribution to the successful success of India's Mars mission. In reality, the film was promoted with Akshay Kumar in a leading role, although it had a stellar female cast, which speaks much about the public's attitude toward women-centric films. Patriarchy is deeply rooted and reflected in its films, at the very roots of Indian society. The movies are seen mainly as a form of escape and therefore cater to the wider male audience. Cinema is driven by companies and film makers do not want to get away from the stereotypes they have established to give women path breaking roles. The viewer also needs to break this vicious cycle of supply and demand through the productive production of progressive films.

Bollywood has witnessed many forms of leading women in its eighty-year history – from the sacrificial mother, or a pleading damsel, to a woman in charge of her own fate. The transition is gradual and long overdue, but motivated women continue to increase their presence at the phone. The success of movies like Tumhari Sulu, NH10, Neerja, Parched, among others, is testimony to this. This shows that actresses can trust them to bring the complete movie. But a lot is to be done, and more empathy and sensitivity to real women and the problems facing them should be demonstrated.

Gender inequalities exist in Bollywood according to a report in 2017. It showed that plots for women are rarely found in the study, titled "The review of gender stereotyping in the Bollywood Movies". Although the female stars are extremely talented. The study analyzes 4,000 films published from 1970 to 2017. In this study, the scientists have found that women's on-screen time is relatively less than men. For women the screen time was just 31.5%, as opposed to 68.5% for male actors. In terms of film occupations, higher levels roles are designated for men. The study found that lower-level positions are for women. A similar pattern was observed for a key role in which women were less central to the plot than men.

Films are one of the biggest shops for women in society, another study has shown. According to the 2012 study entitled Analysis of Hindi women-centered films in India, the stereotypical portrayal of women is a function of historical and cultural facts.

However, Aijaz Khan, filmmaker, pointed out another point. The director of Hamid says that in Indian films the portrayal of women is less due to the male gaze. "For the most part, everything is seen in the male way," he said.

2018 was a year of women's banners. Out of 10 hit movies, seven were female-oriented in the first half of 2018 and Padmaavat was the largest of them. In India, the film was worth Rs 300 crore.

However, success in a box office is not a common case for female-centered films. According to the FICCI-EY study, there were approximately 2,000 film releases in 2017. In Bollywood there were only 12 stories powered by women. And not everyone at the box office could make a mark. On the front of the market, few women's-centered films could attract for themselves a great deal. In fact, Rs 100 crore and above could only make three films. In the last 10 years, only 289 women-centered films were included in the 2017 report. It can be slow to change. But with time, the potential of movies of this genre increases. This is evidenced by the data in the 2017 study. In the 1970s, the proportion of women with central characters in Hindi movies was seven. Between 2015 and 2017, this increased to 11.9%. "In the last three years, during our engagement with the industry, we have seen directors, producers, artists and professionals in the sector push the envelope to create gender-equal cinema. Their cinema is being appreciated and commercially rewarded", Amitabh Behar, CEO of Oxfam India. The audience preference shifts, one aspect which has helped this genre of films gain momentum. "I believe our audiences have always appreciated the film, which gives their characters the depth and the dignity they deserve as far as films with women protagonists are concerned", says Ivan Ayr, director of the film Soni. I think the audience was ready a while ago and probably the movie industry needs to catch up. IMAGO's director is Ayr, who says viewers like Queen, Lipstick under my burkha and Pink have appreciated films. "We need to make the right environment to educate more audience to view lady-oriented films", he said. While Sai believes that "viewers are certainly ready to accept women-centric films, he says for the film industry only success counts. If a female oriented film is a hit at the box office a spate of women- oriented films will follow. Female oriented films will then be considered a Product and a Product which sells is always welcome. In short for the film industry it is business dynamics that counts, he added.

"A ready tolerance of men on all matters by all, including women", Sai says. "By putting out more discourse from women and about women, Khan believes that the situation is going to change". "There have been a handful of films back in the day that have focused on women - like mother India. if only that was done more often", he added. Meanwhile, Chavan said, "Support to regional cinema that supports female point of view through festivals and theatrical release... can bring about a change. I think this small change can impact in large scale because regional cinema has that language of change and people can connect easily with contemporary cinema. So, I think we just need to support them without any kind of discrimination". Keluskar also noted that most of the Indian audience is programmed via TV rather than films and web series. Very that can be altered by lady focused films alone before there is a shift in television (or their services that are syndicated on digital platforms). Compared to TV and Digital, the effect of cinema is negligible in terms of time and convenience.

Another factor that encourages this genre is the success of films with female leaders in international markets. The Phogat sisters, who made their names in the world of wrestling, charmed audiences in China. Dangal focused on this life.

The film's love was so great that over Rs 1,200 crore were collected in this country. One reason the movie was greeted with open arms is the empowerment of women in the neighboring region. For other Indian films, Dangal opened a Chinese film market. In China, Secret Superstar was yet another film based on women's power. The Rs 799 crore was collected in 24 days. It became the most successful foreign film in China in 2018. In the Asian nation, Rani Mukherjee-starrer Hichki also gains hearts. At the Shanghai International Film Festival, she received a standing ovation. On the front in the box-office the film is trendy with a revenue of around Rs 37 crore. The Censor Board, however, must promote women-centered films along with the public and the industry.

Alankrita Shrivastava's Lipstick Under My Burkha has been named by the Central Board of Film Certification (CBFC). Even a certificate was refused until the Appellate Tribunal for Film Certification was introduced.

"The censor board needs to treat these films with the same level of objectivity, without getting taken aback by the content", said Aijaz Khan. "If they can accept sexist content that trivializes women and objectifies them - and they are still okay with this going out, they definitely need to start following a more progressive way of thinking", he added. Ayr had the view, "if there has to be a censor board, then I believe they must not veer away from their ratings guidelines and adhere to a common set of rules for each film that comes their way". "Contemporary film, according to Chavan, is a strong medium for the underlining of society hidden dark secrets and it is necessary for an artist to reflect on society past, present and future. "To be able to do the same fearlessly, one needs freedom. Keeping the primary motto of CBFC intact, they can surely treat contemporary cinema with a wider, liberal perspective."

Director Shrivastava believes there is a need for more female directors to better depict women in films. There are still inequalities as more women are filmmakers coming to the fore. Accommodating just 9% female director, 12% female writers and 15% female producers according to 2014 study by the Geena Davis institute for media genre. These are less than averages worldwide. The study entitled "Cinema in society: shaping our world view through the lens- Indian films" revealed only female one in ten movie directors (9.1 per cent).

Contemporary Indian film industry witnesses the rise of women-centric films. Although gender was a key issue in the new wave cinema, yet its visibility was not so prominent as it seems now. While on one hand, films like Toilet: Ek Prem Katha (Shree Narayan Singh, 2017) or Padman (R. Balki, 2018) have gained considerable attention from the audiences, on the other, Lipstick Under My Burkha (Alankrita Srivastava, 2016) or Lust Stories (Zoya Akhtar, Dibakar Banerjee, Karan Johar, Anurag Kashyap, 2018) have been successful in raising critical debates about the changing gender relation in Indian social context. Filmmakers like Zoya Akhtar, Reema Kagti, Alankrita Srivastava, as well as others have been instrumental in this shift of focus towards questions of gender, agency, masculine anxiety and various trajectories of the cinematic representations of these issues. What is noteworthy is the aggressive presence of diverse digital media platforms that have flooded Indian entertainment market in the wake of economic liberalization and the rise of the IT sector. Among other things that streaming platforms such as Netflix and Amazon have brought in are the new articulations of gender that question, challenge, and at times appear to subvert the patterns of traditional Indian patriarchal systems.

In earlier days, to make a women centric film, they just swapped the male protagonist with a female protagonist. In other cases, they made movies about women being put under the tortures of the society. While one shows the women over powered, the other depicted them very weak. This is the main reason for women centric movies being flop or not well received by the audience. Also, the society was not ready to listen to their sufferings stating that movies are meant to be enjoyed. But in recent times, the change is very obvious.

More number of women centric movies is being released. Among them, most are well received by the audience. This is one of the positive changes that have happened in the recent cinema industry. But at the same time, making women lead as the main character just for attracting audience can be seen in half of the films. This issue can be rectified only when the audience demands character driven women characters instead of beautiful women as female lead.

Figure 1.5: Women centric movies that gained audience appreciation (https://www.shethepeople.tv/news/women-centric-movies-robbed-box-office/)

Body Imaging in Indian Cinema

The previously dominant political environments and societal expectations of the time and culture influenced people's view of the perfect women's body type. The cultural rules of Indian society were followed by films made in India. Woman did not wish to be something other but her social position, where she embodied the continuity of life, a force which could not be separated or divers ionized without a subsequent lack of vitality. No distinction was made between moral and sensual: Indian women did not distort their bodies in the interests of mode; they were more concerned with service than with rights:

More frequently than not, women play the kind of roles on the screen, the male director knows what role women can play. This idea is based on the views, behaviours and ideals of the director, mixed with what the director feels people want to see. The viewer's aspirations are based on his views, behaviours and ideals, which are derived from the social context under which they reside, the same as directors.

The Indian film industry began to adapt to the Western women's image to the audience of the diaspora after liberalization, privatization and globalization (LPG). The styles of actresses chosen to portray women were young and western in nature and were often supposed to fit the Western society's body type and normality. These criteria were focused on the genetic structure of the body focused on a certain geographical area in the country.

Since the early days of cinema, both change and transformation has taken place in the portrayal of women's bodies depicted on film. The body depicted on the screen is affected also by the socio-economic condition of India, whether it is from a voluptuous full bloom figure or from a new trend to the size zero.

Indians have historically claimed that they have good eating patterns and find curved forms of body more attractive because they meant prosperity, stability and family care. The geographical position of India is close to the equator and hence it is a tropical region, which historically needs women to have structures that could have healthy children. This may be one of the reasons why different types of art represent curved female bodies. In the 1940s and 50's, cinema in India mirrored this and claim both dimensions.

Diet and exercise were intended to ensure women adhere to those expectations of appearance which men found desirable. The 19th Century or twentieth Century fad for slimness. Women embraced these ideas, as they brought love, praise and way to the heart of the man. The slim body has been symbolizing consumption, glamour, and sexual availability, and is no longer a result of just an ascetical motivation for redemption. The oddity of sociology not being able to establish an artistic philosophy is emphasized by the popular belief that diet, jogging, fasting, slimming and exercise are no longer just necessary aids in obtaining sexual fulfilment. Present societal expectations of women's beauty highlight slimness and sleekness.

The entertainment industry has taken to the belief that women will attract an audience with transparency clothes. The female character's body parts are displayed as male interest objects through camera angles and by camera framing. In the view of the male performer, from the view of the camera lenses, and from the view of the male observer who stares at the female individual only by viewing her as an object for their sexual needs. The male gaze is a matter of sexual objectification. Under the firm influence of the patriarchy women are bound to accomplish their goals by offering their bodies to the masculine protagonist or, in contemporary films, to a man who is now made and regarded as top-class films around the world for sexual fulfilment. Although such films are made by woman makers, they are often under masculine domination, which simply see woman as an exotic object of their sexual needs in films. This is therefore why the producer only wanted to benefit from the economically generated movies behind the objectification of women's organizations. Therefore, sexual harassment and objective treatment leading to exploitation of women are perceived to be acceptable to females as an entertaining sex object. The fact that films have sexual objectivity inflames sexual harassment, sexual assaults and other forms of violence, including rape.

Moreover, objectification of women body is under the strict ideology of patriarchy. The main targeted audience is male therefore under the invisible domination of men the films are a source for sexual satisfaction and also responsible for wrong temptation and sexual aggression among men in the patriarchal society. Therefore, such a kind of entertainment is actually meant for exploitation of women under patriarchy.

Cosmetically modified bodies are often displayed in mass media and the audience can be informed of the type of body form which is acceptable. This is the main reason behind people's thinness and white skin fascination. They show pictures which promise social acceptance and become a trend later on. The outward behaviour that causes everyone to mold themselves to such false expectations of appearance has been put enormously emphasized.

The patriarchal culture has been overshadowing women for decades. They have never been presented with a medium for establishing their essence, and therefore appear to induce others' expectations and attempt to describe their life in the same manner.

Unlike the retro view of a "full body", women currently regard themselves as beautiful if they have an ounce-fat hourglass figure. The slim and slender ideal is widespread from soap operas and magazines and billboards. Women of all ages compare with models of this kind. Some reality Shows and movies of India enhance this point of view. For certain women, it is not possible because of varying medical problems to reach these types and zero statistics. This adds to an imagery of the body that adds to unhealthy eating and exercise. Women also have anorexia, bulimia, and other related diseases.

In comparison to traditional female actors, slim and curved stars are portrayed as good, socially attractive characters in films. Such a thin body is linked to joy and pleasure. Women undergo processes like botulinum injections, sessional skin clearance, breast augmentation, rhinoplasty, and so forth to follow those flawed values.

Women body is not a public resource that is subject to critique and review. Negative imagery forces an individual to think the reverse, though. Both men and women like to look like individuals whose images spread in the media and hear constructive judgements. People are forced in their own skin to feel uncomfortable.

In the pursuit of a perfect corporeal appearance that fits societal and cultural expectations, people fail to concentrate on creating their artistic talents that will enable them to be a productive part of society. Too much emphasis on outer appearance – for a person or culture – is not helpful. This does not open up for the future and sometimes ends in stagnation. The definition of body photography and advertising attractiveness is not the same as the principle of healthy living. It is ridiculous to describe oneself in terms of beauty.

Today the Indian beauty is a sound, a slippery, fair, tall woman who can bind to and fuse effortlessly with the Western notions of beauty. The presence in West Fashion and Culture of Indian heritage models and heroines is partially responsible for the immense shift in body styles. It should be noted here that in urban women who are highly exposed to international press and lifestyle compared with rural women who are not, the phenomenon for having a slim, slender body is a bit limited. The Western ideal of thinness seems to have influenced the most advanced and westernized regions of the world, with both backward and rural areas appearing to remain the same, considering the large variation of their culture and customs. These values are mostly forced on the society by the actors and actresses in Indian Cinema. The decision to not eat entails a power of surplus production which only the privileged or well-off classes enjoy.

Cultural Impact and Stereotypes

Most books claim unwaveringly that Indian cinema remains under-examined academically, despite its size, linguistic variety and social influence. This argument is irrelevant from the contemporary influence of the media. The film industry in Hindi is also a melting pot of cultures and an example of Indian secularism. True, but the cinema of Hindi is not politically innocent or unmistakably secular; its "social" film is based on a politics of inequality and escapism. Hindi cinema is reactionary in matters of sex, reason, science and modernization. It also maximized the vulgar in order to optimize returns. Some volumes, like The Cinemas of India, are encyclopedic and remind us that Hindi is not the only a language in which numerous Indian films are made. They are important to readers unfamiliar with Indian cinema.

It would be wrong to assume this trend is totally new. In the early decades of Indian independence, globalization is focused on foundations of modernization. Nehruvian educational and industrial institutions are the source of the confidence of the middle class. Another stage of bourgeois hegemony in India is the domination of the Indian media by globalization. In Indian cinema there were first class and caste statements. Lifestyles that valued in the 1950s and 1960s were the businessman's, with exceptions. The well-designed houses were not available to most of the audiences. It even seemed amazing to a police inspector's home. Debonair's heroes drove their "westoxicated" parents to expensive imported cars. The women were traditional and patriarchal. Their destiny was marriage. The mode was west in these male westernization appropriations. There was glorified access to the west; many films had airport scenes. In the Indian context, the Indian bourgeois male westward (read the modernity) In these films liberated women, white as well as Indian, endangered Indian families' solidarity. His story was underscored by the protagonists' associations in class, caste, religion and regional affiliation, visiting Kashmir, Paris and even Tokyo, pursuing romance, adventure and business. Thus, the Hindi per- globalization film established and colonized the mainstream.

In popular Indian films in the context of growing social unrest, there is growing trend for sex and violence. The disgruntled young man who takes up the task of fighting the unjust capitalist structure for the downtrodden substituted the heroic character from the 1960s and the beginning of the 1970s. The criminalization of the role of a woman is also romanticized as a reaction to women's injustices in their lives. Incorrectly, then, the avenging hero is the excuse for the brutal gory. The heroine role is decorative and secondary for building the hero's macho image. Actually, the vamps used for the dark side of modernity in earlier films vanished more or less from popular Indian cinema. This is the protagonist who is both a seductive dancer and singer who at the same time draws the hero and a "good" woman who sustains patriarchal norms.

The hero remained young, equitable, beautiful, eligible, romantic, fixed mother, upper caste, north Indian and preferably richer in male-centered Hindi cinema. Heroes start with poor high caste men in many movies, but end up wealthy. Films had happy endings-never did the plots go incorrect. Most movies may have a bad protagonist but not a Christian, Sikh or Muslim individual in general.

This was clearly defined by Surnames and the hierarchy of characters. The genteel poverty was shown by unfavorable conditions often created by evil in property managers or families. The true poor, like dalits or adivasis, were never the center subject. The movies that differed from this plot were uncommon, such as Do Bigha Zamin or Sahib Biwi Ghulam. Patriarchy was promoted by mainstream Bombay cinema in the 50s and 60s as predominantly Indigenous. Women could be slapped off as little as illumination! Run minorities flourished in non-Hindu plots. Historical and Muslim social characters dominated. In those social events, there was a stereotype Muslim ambiance in Barsaat ki Raat, Mere Mehboob, Ghazaly Mer Huzoor (my beloved Master in Urdu is frequently called one's superior). With excellent music, songs and "mushaira" these films essentialized the feudal Muslims, with the implication that they were anti-modern Muslims, were always the Hindustani, former "nawabs" and "zamindar" and "jagirdars" in their own right. All spoke chaste Urdu, wearing 'sherwani,' loving 'shaayari.' These films are difficult to find, given the urban Hindustan culture that quickly declined after independence. These films can be easily located.

The stereotyping of positive and negative groups and castes, which excels in Hindi film, emphasizes the process of "smaller" and reduces the distance between communalism, Casteism and nationalism. Not all. Tradition and Westernization were part of a perception of modernity that informed the bourgeois world view in India. The Nation State imagined was patriarchal. This paper demonstrates why and how Hindi cinema has become a way of getting modernization into harmony with conventional constraints. The middle-class ideas of gender, sexuality, caste, region and religion provided the pivots on which this reconciliation moved. All of them should be divided into topics acceptable in the third world circumstances to the bourgeois and the poor, or else the nation would disintegrate as the political and cultural emblem of bourgeois hegemony.

Cultural Hegemony

Hegemony is the political, economic, ideological, or cultural power that dominates other groups by a dominant group. The effect of hegemony is huge on what is depicted by the TV. Press domination encourages people to accept the status quo that includes structures of power so that the medium class has more control over the working class. The most important theory Gramsci used to deal with was the relationship between culture and power under capitalism. The notion of cultural hegemony is given by Antonio Gramsci. Gramsci studies have almost often described his work as an attempt to loosen orthodox Marxism's rigidity. No definite description of cultural hegemony is found in the translated writing of Gramsci. The nearest thing to that is his frequently cited hegemony as the 'spontaneous' consent given by the great masses of the population to the general direction imposed on social life by the dominant fundamental group; this consent is 'historically' caused by the prestige (and consequent confidence) which the dominant group enjoys because of its position and function in the world of production". Gramsci thought that the media have always played a major role in encouraging people to do things that help power structures in their everyday lives. It is seen in the media how power structures like governments, capitalists, and patriarchy are supported. The philosophy of domination by Gramsci does not only allow one to grasp the reasons behind discriminatory media pictures. It also forms part of a key process to show that White 'liberal' reforms are not sufficient. Even though racial minorities are well intended, the white hegemony of media production means that TV and cinema are still subjugating these social groups.

Hegemony is a concept coined from the Marxist intellectual Antonio Gramsci, and developed from Marxist writings. Throughout the nation, the capitalist class maintains its supremacy by the cultural and financial unity that corporations, political groups, colleges, the newspaper, the church and other voluntary organizations enforce. Gramsci talks about the cycle of "False Awareness" that contributes to social domination and coercion through generating expectations and choices. This process explains how people, media and information organization controls the thinking and actions that create a state of rule by creating dominant ideologies. The cultural hegemony and it's inter connections are shown in Figure 1.6.

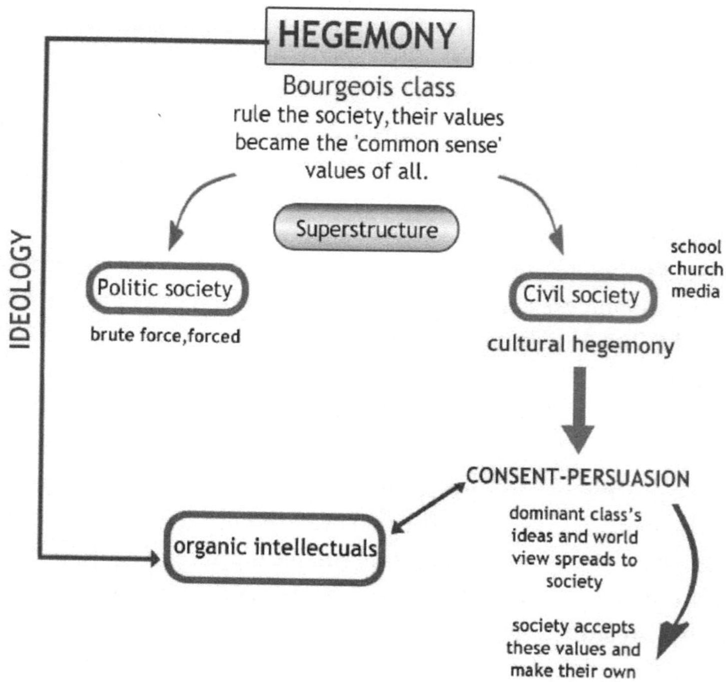

Figure 1.6: Structure of culture hegemony (https://www.slideshare.net/elma22/politics-and-cultureantonio-gramsci)

In this theory, cinema has a major role in particular because ideology is at the center of fighting for ideas and views. Due to its importance and control over the citizens, the role of film is significant in the theory of hegemony. For culture to behave in a consumerist manner, cinema serves as a tool. In this situation, film is the force that teaches them and leads them to consumption. This is where the film's role as an ideological instrument leads to ideological leadership and control in film. A concentrated film industry allows media companies to exercise an expanded impact on popular sentiment and the absence of plurality in viewpoints, beliefs and opinions.

The problem arises when the media is in control while the revolutionary discourse is frequently picked up and re-constructed in the mainstream media to re-establish the dominant social classes' supremacy and to recreate ties between men and women, women's organizations and media workers remain threatened within a larger system that dominates the mainstream media and excludes women.

Mass media coverage for the majority of women in the third world is far from easy because of factors like analphabetism, inaccessibility, household replacement, uncomfortable programs, and traditional restrictions on their mobility to theater or the movies. The position of mainstream media is still paramount in upholding social values and ideologies throughout the country.

Many philosophers and writers have mentioned these same issues that have existed in some other form through their works. Karl Marx has contributed in sharing his own point of view in cultural hegemony and feminism. Marxist Feminism as it stands strictly perceives patriarchy, a society characterized by male domination over women, in terms of capitalism. Marxist Feminism focuses specifically on the roles that capitalism designates to women in the production process and the harmful implications this has. The philosophical variant of feminism is Marxist feminism which integrates and expands Marxist theory. Marxist feminism analyses how women are oppressed by patriarchy and by private land ownership. The enlightenment of females can be accomplished only through demolishing the capitalist systems that hold a lot of female work, according to Marxist feminists. Marxist feminists broaden conventional Marxist analysis to unpaid housework and sex.

Like Marx, Althusser was inspired by Freud and Lacan in his theory of ideology. Capitalism, he claims, gives the idea that we are autonomous people who chose, but our interests, decisions, expectations (including three others) for him are the product of the social practices that we have internalized in society. He stresses the role of ideology in allowing the capitalist classes to use the state in their control of the working classes. In Marxist tradition, Althusser says, the State is regarded as an apparatus of repression which enables the ruling class to retain its domination over the working class. Althusser provides a feminist ideological analysis denied by traditional Marxism.

Bourdieu criticized a lot of theoretical and analytical work through his work. Bourdieu (1985)'s social space architecture reflects on the idea of capital: "The structure of the social world is defined at every moment by the structure and distribution of the capital and profits characteristic of the different particular fields" and it is important to work out the correct hierarchy "of the different forms of capital". Capital refers to social agents' multiple sources of influence. In Bourdieu, different types of capital (power) are defined, including fiscal, social, cultural, symbolic, language, educational and corporeal. Bourdieu says that women are normally not subjects that accumulate money. Rather, they are "capital bearing objects" whose meaning is derived from their primary groups (for example, their husband, their family). This same screening of women in movies was introduced. They are only used as the revenue input for venture capital. This exact projection was implemented on women in cinema. They are just viewed as the input for income to the capital investment.

The essence of hegemonic masculinity, as a sociological term, stems from the Marxist theorist Antonio Gramsci's theory of cultural hegemony, which analyses the relations of dominance between the social groups of a society.

Hegemonic masculinity is part of Connell's theory of gender order in gender studies, which acknowledges various masculinities that differ across time, culture and the individual. Hegemonic masculinity is characterised as a practise that legitimises the superior status of men in society and defends subordination and other marginalised forms of becoming a man to the common male population and women. Conceptually, hegemonic masculinity seeks to justify how and why men have dominant social roles over women and other gender identities that are viewed in a given society as "feminine".

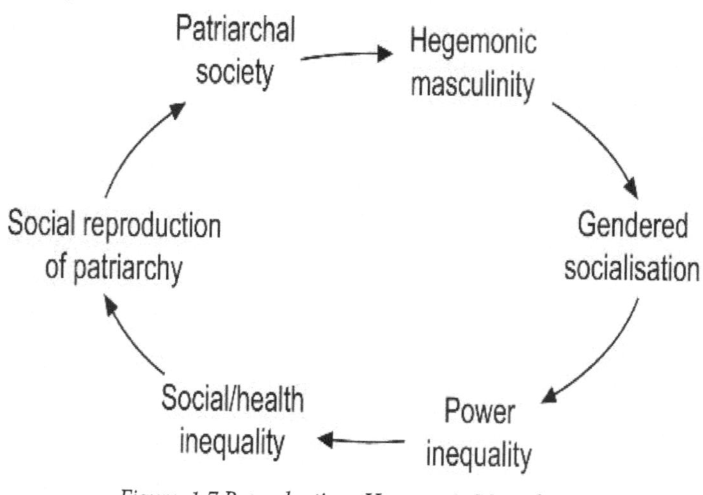

Figure: 1.7 Reproductions Hegemonic Masculinity (https://www.google.com/search?q=hegemonic+masculinity)

Here Socialization/ culture play major roles for shaping the behaviour of individuals in society. These cultures (Culture consists of a set of principles and traditions that are passed on from generation to generation) values is inculcate in human being through socialization process. Socialization helps shape and defines our thoughts, feelings and actions, and gives us a role model. When children socialize, they begin to blend into and function when active members of society.

Socialization teaches us the universal principles and expectations that direct our day-to-day lives. In the family there is primary socialization. In other social bodies, including the school system, peer circle, newspapers, culture and the working environment, secondary socialization is carried out outside the home.

Many thinkers told us about the role of socialization on our life through the help of their theory like "looking glass self" by cooley and 'theory of "I" and "Me", by Mead. They are basically discussed how society is important in our life because we are all product of this. Even Durkhime also put the society in the center of his discourse.

So here the basic fact to discuss the above is that society teaches us culture and values through socialization. 'A girl should behave like a girl' and 'a boy should behave like boy', all these values are taught to us in the society thorough the socialization for example if a boy cries then people make fun of him saying 'why is crying like a girl', because crying is girl's behaviour not boy. Whereas such values and norms are generated by society and we are taught throughout our life through socialization.

The result of gender socialization can be the gender stereotypes. Girls and boys will behave in such respects, and much of their parents (and society) socialize from birth. Decision-makers can make use of this framework to shape their efforts in the development of policies and programs aimed at increasing gender equality, understanding key areas and actors they can influence and contribute to, and constructing a broader theory of change. But if media such as movies take this into their own hands, they can change its characteristics, however they like.

There are various kinds of Patriarchy among us. We frequently define patriarchy as an oppressive structure, aimed mainly at women, while patriarchy is in fact a structure under which we are all oppressed irrespective of the sex identity (which is anyway a social structure). We are both the oppressor and the victim in this system. Yet sexism does not often be seen or perceived as a measurable object. Inequality also operates in so many respects that the underlying inequality is not recognized in it. So that's much more sinister because it renders us a part of our own injustice. This system is mirrored in our everyday behaviour, thoughts, beliefs, festivals and rites, etc. Mythologies, folk tales, legends, and allegories play a very important role here, especially in cinemas. Such movies express not only narratives, but also philosophical arguments by way of symbols and abstract representations. We bring universal ideals, and societal expectations such that they are part of our life and find their way through our society, through our unconscious mind.

Popular visual imagery is viewed as a challenge from 'modernity' to the 'home and conservative people' ideal. Therefore, 'western' west-looking women in our famous movies are seldom shown in good light. They demonstrate that either they are "loose" or "sexually promiscuous" or that they are "manipulative and aggressive," attributes that are contradictory to "simplicity and obedience" attributes of a 'typical' individual. Although films also offer women selective organizations, there are almost no TV shows that do not support and affirm the 'traditional Indian family' and its values. Throughout the "private domain" of the home, people, too, seldom play any part.

Of course, there is a patriarchal structure, but there is a protest against this dominant structure simultaneously at a more modest level, however. It also implies, though, that masculinity is in essence a great system to contend with through alternate systems. We don't even realize that the main problem with resisting patriarchy is the same. The system we seek to avoid is what we exist under. Thus, we have some effect on patriarchal systems through our devices, strategies and concepts to combat patriarchal. Not only does film reinforce in the most efficient manner possible the patriarchal values and the injustice associated with these norms are subconsciously normalized. So that's why cinema is so strong so risky.

Women's status in India has changed a lot over the recorded history of India. In ancient India, particularly in the Indo-Aryan-speaking regions, their role in society deteriorated early and their subordination remains quite strongly matured into early contemporary India. Practices like female children's infanticide, child marriage, widow remarriage and dowry have been long-term in India and have proved to be difficult to get rid of, particularly in northern Caste Hindu society. The privileges of women under the Indian Constitution include, in particular, liberty, independence and the freedom to discriminate; furthermore, India has numerous laws regulating women's rights. Several reformers like Ishwar Chandra Vidyasagar, Jyotirao Phule and Ram Mohan Roy have been battling for the empowerment of women under British Raj.

In this context, Foucault mostly talks about women very passively. A major contribution to feminist criticism of essentialism was Foucault's theory that body and sexuality are societal constructions, rather than inherent phenomena. Foucault seems to have been somewhat sympathetic to feminism, but he didn't place any kind of analysis of gender or sex even remotely central to his work. The main thing Foucault contributed to feminism was a lengthy exploration of how power operates. These power holders are the ones who decide what a woman can have.

India has also been the "fourth most dangerous country" for women worldwide; India has also been recognized as the worst country in the G20 countries for women but critiques for promoting incorrect perceptions have been made in this report. Rajya Sabha approved the Women's Reservation Bill on 9 March 2010, one day after International Women's Day, requiring that 33 percent of India's parliamentary and government legislative bodies be reserved for women.

In India, women's status is closely linked to families. Throughout India, the family is considered as important and the family structure is patrilineal in most sections of the world. Families are hereditary, the wife is going to stay with the attorneys. Families typically have dominant control over the younger generations, and men over women. In India, however, polygyny and polyandry have a long tradition between certain peoples, and most marriages are single (one husband, one wife).

Since 2018, certain female officials in India have held various senior positions, such as that of Indian Prime Minister, India's President, and the President of the Lok Sabha government. However, many women still face major difficulties in India. The levels of malnutrition among adolescents and pregnant and lactating women in India are extraordinarily large, with implications on the wellbeing of children. There has been an increasing number of violence against women, including sexual violence, in India. Almost the ideology was presented by Baudrillard. He has evoked both furious rejections and complex evaluations in his mid-works views of gender and in particular his formulation of the Nietzschean-Derridean concept of the woman. The debate about feminism, philosophy of critique and politicization more broadly is raised by Baudrillard. He was focusing on detecting a fundamental issue at the core of gender philosophy, demonstrating that the latter capitalist plight of sign society is more encompassing of the obituary of dissent. Their dedication was not so much to gender as a spiritual and representative challenge, as to take up this challenge in the sense of an environmental crisis that jeopardizes the contemporary ambition to reflect truthfulness and meaningfulness in itself.

Now we have women drivers of buses, subway drivers, drivers, posters, flying squads, pilots, scientists, and so on. Women have told the planet simply that they are powerless to overcome everything. They took over men's strongholds and made themselves effective. Females are decision leaders now. They have a lot of women in our nation's presidents and prime ministers. In other critical instances women governed the nation and proved themselves to be the strongest decision leaders in crises. Women in power steal the light and make their decisions respected by men. They have their own version of media through which their views can be shared with the whole world.

There are many Indian cinema released till today. Every movie affects us in one way or other. They have the potential to change mindset of society. So, whatever is presented in cinema has to be made sure that it has positive effect on the society. The way of treatment, the mannerisms shown in cinemas are followed by many youths in India. Cinema can even change the course of a generation of people. As cinema has this much of influence on society and culture, there need to be a proper understanding of what are the positive things that should be attained and what

the concept of marriage, male gaze, questions of feminine morality, marginal role of Muslim women in Hindi movies are explored in 24 essays by different writers.

Global Bollywood establishes relationship with the global market between Hindi movies popularly referred to as 'Bollywood.' Film which is a cultural development, and a symbol of the nation "India" has not only been the cross-country culture within the world. The book explores many factors which made it possible to engage with the world market. Vamsee Juluri's essay 'Our Violence, Their Violence' provides a detailed meditation on the brutality in the Hindi films.

Ganti Tejaswini explores in Chapters 3 and 4 the plot structure, key topics, and common genre of Indian film in Bollywood : A Guidebook to Popular Hindi Cinema' (2013). She also said that there are three prevalent topics of Hindi films. The heroes of the former and the villains of the latter are good versus bad, right versus injustice and responsibility versus wish. The chapters thus helped everyone to explore various forms of pessimistic characters in Hindi cinema. In an essay "Pleasing Both Aunties and Servants: The Hindi Film Industry and Its Audience Imaginaries", another book by the same author, 'Producing Bollywood Inside the contemporary Hindi Film Industry' (2012), provides an overview of the Hindi film industry, its styles, their preferences and its aspirations.

Gulzar, Govind Nihalani & Saibal Chatterjee's 'Encyclopedia of Hindi Cinema' (2003) gives an insight into different film-making aspects: songs and dance, special effects, stunts and action, text and sound etc. The book contains three essays written by filmmaker specialists. It's an entertaining and informative high-quality reference book. This also addresses the trading power of this sector and its enterprise. In addition to addressing films and their trends and methodologies, it also provides a detailed biography of the actors and actresses who contributed valuably to Hindi films. The essay 'Heroes and Villains: Good versus Evil' provides a short but exact history of villagers' types. In his essay 'Rebels without Cause, Indian Feminism, Rao Maithili talks of negative female personalities in Hindi films.

The essays on Mumbai and its characteristics from the perspective of scholars, writers and campaigners include essays by Sujata Patel and Jim Masselos (2003) on the "Bombay and Mumbai : The City in Transition". It talks about the lives of urban and rural people in the town. It offers insight into your struggle and your sorrow. 'Slums: The Continuous Struggle for Housing' by P.K. This is a comment on how government policies and politics make the lives of slum inhabitants miserable. After the 1992-93 Hindu-Muslim uprisings, Jyoti Punwani presents an image of Mumbai. Ganger Amrit addresses the reasons of the studio system's collapse and the challenge of underworld bribery in 'Tinseltown: From Studios to Industry'. He claims that the policy of the government that saved Hindi film from underworld mafia clashes to assign it an industry status. In "Satya's Mumbai, Mumbai's Satya"

Pendse Sandeep provides a contrast between the real Satya Mumbai and Mumbai, and therefore includes an exploration of the kind of underworld don films.

The subject guide for students in film studies is the 'doing film studies' by Sarah Casey Benyahia and Claire Mortimer. For beginners in this area, the book is a must read. They have listed to reassure themselves of the link between films and literature. The book offers information on different methodologies for the study of films; the philosophy of the image, film psycho analysis and feminist film philosophy. It also addresses numerous methods for analyzing films. An audience chapter talks about film theories developed with the audience in mind.

'Making Significance in Indigenous Cinema' is a series of essays written by Ravi S. Vasudevan which discuss politics in films. Vasudevan shows his frustration with the kind of melodramatic movies he has made in his essay 'Shifting Codes, Dissolving Identities,' the filmmaking is more intense and more practical. The tradition of adding music and dance scenes is disapproved of. He also suggests that the viewer should be trained to view films on such a critical story. Lalita Gopalan addressed the topic of rape vengeance, the reasons for her fame, and the politics behind this theme's presentation in her essay "Avenging women in Indian cinema". "From Subjectification to Schizophrenia: The Angry Man and the Psychotic Hero of Bombay Cinema" is a thorough analysis of the characteristics of Angry Young Man and anti-heroes. The characters are examined in a detailed fashion.

The Art of Entertaining Millions essay from Naseer Munni Kabir in 'Bollywood: The Indian Cinema Story' (2001) highlights the latest trends in Hindi film and discusses the effects of globalization in Hindi cinema presentations.

'Cinema India: the visual history of Hindi cinema' by Rachel Dwyer and Divya Patel (2002, 2002) focuses on the factors that enhance the visual impact in Hindi films such as songs and dance. The book commentates in various ways on heroes, heroines, peasants and vamps, as these characters characterize Indian visual culture, which governs their images very strongly.

'Bollywood Baddies' (2013) by Ghosh is a book completely devoted to Hindi film guides, vamps and fans. The analysis of pessimistic characters has been significantly improved. The book illustrates socio-political structural developments that have often altered the representation of derogatory characteristics. Not just the actors and actresses who play negatory roles on the film, but also their personalities and life off the film. It includes them. The novel is thus not monotonous. The book is an outstanding study of negative traits done with great insight.

The personality of the pessimistic personalities of Alsford's 'Heroes and Villain' (2006) was analyzed in detail. This explores the heroes 'and peasants' traits and tries to demonstrate parallels and differences that make up these two contrasting characters.

'Subject: Cinema, Object woman', Chatterji's (1998) book includes two essays 'The Politics of Rape' and "From Hunterwali to Bandit Queen Women in Male Masquerade" which address the real purpose behind Hindi and Hollywood films of woman avengers.

Lucy Nevitt addresses the viewing of violence on the stage and its influence on the viewer in Theater & Terrorism. Her review of her book has made me appreciate the sort of violence that films display and its impact on the viewer.

"Bollywood and Globalization Indian Popular Cinema", "Nation and Diaspora" (Rini Bhattacharya Mehta et.al.) has a Chaudhry Purna article which discusses the market changes in Hindi films, with examples of the negative characters of women: Mohara, Darr and Aitraaz. She also written on the depiction of women sexuality in Hindi films in her post. She believes that the exposure of the female body by heroines should not be considered as something derogatory because of globalization when Hindi films are also seen by the Diaspora. In comparison, it should be seen as a cultural shift which, while within limits, encourages women to explore their sexuality.

Although the clear connection between viol in real life and rape in films is difficult to prove, studies have repeatedly shown that rape media material frequently forms the concept of rape in the audience (Ramasubramanian and Oliver 2003). The rape's trivialization overlooks the horrific nature of rape, and in turn helps perpetuate the rape myth over time.

The work submitted by the university student on "Representation of Women in Hindi Cinema Film" (UKEssays, 2018) shows the situation as it is. Indian culture and community have also seen Hindi cinema as a significant influence. It has not only formed, but has also articulated the shifting situations and contours of India's social and cultural feelings in such a way that no other art form has ever been successful. Hindi movie has been influential in perceiving and coping with diverse facets of their own lives.

'From Reverence to Rape: The Treatment of Women in the Movies' by Molly Haskell (1974) was perhaps the first book to write on women's suffering in movies. She evaluates films in her dissertation as a by-product of culture as well as a moral arbiter and claims they are deeply rooted in the inferiority of women. She further explores how prejudices stay focused on people who are depicted as fictitious characters who are not authentically remembered.

It is important to examine improvements and modifications in celluloid females' projection in Hindi films and how it aids in woman objectification. Mulvey's essay "Visual and other Pleasures" in 1975 explores the relationship between psychoanalysis and film drawing on Althussian, Lacanian, and Freudian trends in art theory. There, she examines how masculinity builds films from the viewpoint of the male gaze, like how women function as a "see-seeing thing" through voyeuristic or fetishism structures that minimize the danger of otherness. We condemn women as the "other" in which status is established within the patriarchal system. The belief that women are objects in movies comes out of this. Her emphasis lies on how the sexual disparity in classical cinema is replicated.

The arguments against the omnibus patriarch's dominance are the de-construction of the suffocating role of phallocentric society found in myths and criticisms of the social ties that represent the identity of women in "Femininity and Domination: Studies in the Phenomenology of Oppression" (1990). Bartky tries to examine in her book several modes of consciousness which are 'feminine' as oppressed by patriarchal domination: narcissism feminine and masochism, feminine emotional work, sexual self-objection and selflessness. He also argues for a reform of the structures of influence, as they threaten the role of women in society.

The topic of cinema (1990), by Gaston Roberge, illustrates the main ideas of film theory followed by a thorough account of the transformation from an idealistic model of thinking to a materialistic model which took place around the mid-60s as part of intellectual revolution. Gaston's research provides a revived notion of film theory from a theoretical context- Structures, Marxism and Feminism, semiotics, psychoanalysis and linguistics. In "Film Art: An Introduction" (1990) David Kristin and Thompson Bordwell gave a straightforward account of film making, film structure (narrative and narrative), art forms that define the scene of films and videos, critical analyzes of film genres and film history to explain the important growth and progress in films.

Dissanayake and K. Wimal and K. The historical and cultural aspects of Bollywood are given in Gokulsing's "Indian Popular Cinema: A Narrative of Cultural Change" (1998). The author attempts to deliver a descriptive and encyclopedic guide to Indian cinema by highlighting important themes, subjects, movies and figures in Indian film. In the advent of the novel, an outline of Indian film's historic growth, main features and distinctive facets were expanded, and an analysis of crucial topics and issues was accompanied by a review of a wide range of films. In fact, the misconceptions of women in Indian films have been discussed in one of the pages.

The film critic's contributions in the study of Indian cinema with the aid of feminist film theory, Shoma Chatterjee in the subject of "Cinema Object: Woman: A Study of the Portrayal of women in Indian Cinema" (1998). Her research explores main topics from the perspective of an Indian woman and her film depiction, including religion, incest, murder, abortion, marriage, suicide and masquerade. In a similar vein the role of women in the Indian society and their onscreen representation 'Roles: Reel and Real: Image of Woman Hindi Cinema' by Manjiri Prabhu (2001). A Bollywood comprehensive research explores the 'why s and how s' in Hindi films with the various complexities in celluloid females.

M. Madhava Prasad presents the Hindi cinema from the Marxist viewpoint in his work "Ideology of the Hindi Cinema: A Historical Construction" (1998), implying it to be an intellectual development center. Prasad explores the prevalent texts of modern cinema as a means of development, acceptance and repetition of the predominant ideology and the portrayal of ideology in the social structure, taking as their basis the conceptions of dominant ideology, hegemony and the ISAs. They also analyzes the history and the origins of film making, censorship, television and entertainment in a modern culture. Prasad believes that film technology has been developed to fulfill economic, political and social needs currently in life. A comprehensive study of Indian film history from a silent period featuring the most influential movies makers, well-known stars, and notable composers, Ashish Rajadhayaksha and Paul Willeman's 'Encyclopedia of Indian Cinema' (1999). The book suggests a way to look at significant archives — how to look at films from historical points of view as films haven't always existed and even the relevant material is sparse, scattered and often conflicting.

Reconfiguring the conceptions of identity and role and the creation of independent institutions leading to evolving gender-based interactions between all socially-builded relationship communities in contemporary cultures' (2000) is the latest subject of Lois McNay's 'Gender and Agency: Reconfiguring the Subject in Feminist and Social Theory'. The constructionist theory of subjectification is reaffirmed by McNay in reference to plays by such primary thinkers as Pierre Bourdieu, Paul Ricoeur, Judith Butler, Nancy Fraser etc. Their primary point is to step away from the ideas of Foucault and Lacan, as their theorization provides a pessimistic Agency model that limits change away from control and opposition, and create a new understanding of individual agency.

"Globalization and Representation of Women in Indian Cinema" (2000) by Sangeeta Datta examines the effect of political movements in Indian cinema on their mechanism of gender representation. Datta analyzes the effect of world-film, particularly European films and Hollywood, in Indian cinema in the research of dynamics between western and local films as she points out, Indian filmmakers have given a voice to women in Indian cinema, emphasizing the creation of Eurasian actors, and implying that they can help to break up the prevailing patriarchal narrative.

'Bollywood Cinema: Temples of Desire' (2002) by Vijay Mishra analyzes Indian film in two aspects, from a post-colonial analysis and philosophy of movies. From a National and International perspective, Mishra analyzes Indian films like Devdas,

Mother India, Khalnayak, Ram Lakhan, and other, cultural and esthetic identities, and the development of epic history, history and implications of Indian Diaspora. Focusing on women's portrayals in Indi (Hindi) cinema, Mishra states that celluloid females in Bollywood don't want to appear like a vulnerable subject or voyeuristic object in their portrayals. We want instead to be represented as independent, bold protagonists.

The narrative of Indian cinema from a postcolonial theory analyzed by Lalitha Gopalan's "Cinema of Interruptions: Genres of Action in Contemporary Indian Cinema" (2002) points out that there are three types of interruptions; "censorship," intervals, and song sequences, and regulations. She underlines how censoring, when discussing 'avenging women' films from 1990, 'reload the joy of the spectator,' arguing that cycles change cinema and the affirmation of patriarchy, makes such films simply a replication of Western films.

The relationship that existed among "nation" and post-Independent Hindi movies was discussed by Jyotika Virdi in The Cinematic Imagination: Indian Popular Films as Social History (2003). By projecting the Hindi cinema, it says Indian history and national politics as the main body of society. Virdi scrutinizes about thirty films since the 1950s and reveals not just the country's past, but also analyzed the role of women as a result of the anti-colonial tendencies, a storehouse of the local culture to differentiate between and conquer the riches of the West.

Manjunath Pendakur's 'Indian Popular Cinema: Industry, Ideology and Consciousness' (2003) examines the cultural study of popular movies. He says from an Indian cinema female portrayal point of view, that while many representations of women are depicted on television, one aspect to be remembered is that they are meant to be a symbol of attractiveness, desirable and sensual. No matter the roles she plays, she is usually a desired object for men. He also guarantees that the Hindi films require female stars of a slim figure, prominent features and a fair skin. She says that films favor 'young faces' to the elderly actress who is actually 'totalizing male libido,' and tells them the other way around.

"Post feminism: Cultural Texts and Theories" (2009) by Stéphanie and Benjamin reflects the progressive maturation of feminist thought from opposition to post-feminist micro-politics. The work is a response to the earlier existing radical wave of feminism and focuses on the limiting of feminism in second wave in relation to class, race and sexuality. This addresses predecessors, ideas and controversies around post-feminism focused on numerous subjects such as Girl Power and Chick fiction, Postmodern, Third Wave Feminism, Backlash, and Queer Feminism and much more. Post feminism as a transitional moment is suggested and addressed by femininity and sexuality to empower women, using them as a way of self-expression and self-assertion.

Angela McRobbie analyzes the forms in which mainstream culture has been used to dismantle female wealth in “The Aftermath of Feminism: Gender, Culture and Social Change” (2009). She claims that the newspapers was a significant source of interpretation of social norms and social concepts on feminist values. This provides particular explanations of how sexism in mass culture is “undone.” Her key point is that feminism is distorted by its portrayal as a set and frightening force in the historical context. Furthermore, she concludes that young women in popular culture no longer need the patriarchal rhetoric and suggests that the hour is needed in post- feminist contexts.

“Films and Feminism: Essays in Indian Cinema” (2009) by Jasbir Jain and Sudha Rai is a collection of Indian cinemas, presenting women in it, defying their patriarchal rule, and extending their path towards self-discovery. In this research paper the philosophy of cinema, the portrayal of women as victims, revolutionaries and transgressors, camera head, the interconnection between desire, lust, the liberty and the right to the body are the subject matter. Issues such as illnesses, crimes, marriages outside the family and how they are handled are often discussed in film. The book focuses primarily on Indian cinema and emphasizes the value of films that not only reflect reality but construct it by affecting the viewer.

The ties between the current phenomenon of empowered women and the patriarchal society she promotes are explored in ariel Levy’s “Female Chauvinist Pigs: Women and the Rise of Raunch Culture” (2006). She explains how chauvinist pigs create sex symbols to gain dominance in the androcentric world. She asserts in this work, that raunch culture is selling to young women and girls “pseudo power, false liberation and fake rebellion rather than the real thing: freedom.” Women are supposed to be discharged more than ever in order to become more dominant. Therefore, it demonstrates how women deprive of the values of freedom and pride and fear of such hypersexual behaviour.

The 1950-1910, joint research of Dadasaheb Phalke’s Raja Harishchandra, ‘Mother Maiden Mistress: Women in Hindi Cinema’ journeys from 1950 to 2010. They strive to make the women who influenced the movie, style, culture and creativity of the world of celluloid live. In addition, this book is an important contribution because of the early stories of important heroines like Waheeda Rehman, Asha Parekh, Hema Malini, Shabana Azmi, Madhuri Dixit and Rani Mukherjee.

“Routledge Handbook of Indian Cinemas” (2013) by Gokulsing and Wimal Dissanayake reflects Indian cinema’s historical and thematic style. The historical section analyzes Indian cinema’s social, economic, cultural, political and religious contexts, while the critical narratives on large subjects such as viewership, the diaspora, censorship, film production, industry and nationalism and music are discussed in the thematic section. In addition to the growth of Bollywood, it involves a thorough review of Common, Parallel and Regional movies.

Nikita Ramkissoon highlights the success and the misrepresentation of women in Bollywood films, in "Representations of Women in Bollywood Cinema: Characterization, Songs, Dance and Dress in Yash Raj Films from 1997 to 2007". She suggests that in Indian films women were only seen as wallpapers. Things relating to masculinity, femininity, sexuality, discrimination against women on the grounds of class and justice for women tend to be ignored.

In her study, "Gender Reflections in Mainstream Hindi Cinema", Nidhi Shendurnikar Tere notes that the cinema is a pervasive mass medium that plays a prominent role in shaping attitudes, reviving images and impinging on the mainstream customs. Starting with a detailed discussion on the critique of feminist films followed by a mainstream presentation of femininity, the paper discusses the stereotypical representation of female characters in Indian films. Nidhi calls for celluloid characters to be active actors in the final part of the paper so they can deconstruction of the previous power structures, redefining women as subjects of male attention, and creating their own role and identity within the framework of power.

The theme song of Bollywood Lagaan (2001) is studied by Sundar Pavitra Meri Awaaz Suno: Girls, Vocality and the Country in Hindi Cinema in order to see how the voices of singer's playback are the sites of creating a national identity. For more than four decades Lata Mangeshkar monopolized female playback, which has been regarded as the true expression of Indian femininity. A saccharine, ultra-feminine Mangeshkaresque voice with two female choirs one sensual and rough, the other soft and airy is juxtaposed in the Lagaan tune. The diverse women's voices reflect a spectrum of social, domestic and ethnic importance, evoking an egalitarian, democratic India. Yet people with "racial" and physically suggestive voices are still deemed unsafe and not permitted to talk for (or sing) the country in Lagaan's egalitarian society and definitely within the movie industry and wider social milieux the social standards ingrained in the singing voices of Lagaan therefore show the limitations which the voices of the country have in the Hindi film music and vice versa.

Chakraborty has provided an essay that aims at looking at Indian, from the perspective of creation and the other through consummation / appreciation, from the stereotyping of sculpted and decorated bodies. From two separate perspectives. From the outset, it must be explained that by de-stereotyping, he implies not only breaking away from beauty standards, but also moving away from our usual perception of attractiveness which has a history and taking into consideration both the human body and its portrayal as a whole from a culturally significant viewpoint.

With respect to sculpted bodies of ancient India as well as our current historiography of the same, he would like to point out that our present understandings which have been developed in various discourses have typified such art works and brought into being a second level of typicality. It is critical that we ask some concerns regarding our perception of the past's patron consumer partnership and rethink the (male) look and inclination for women's eyes. Yet I do not accept that coding is in the past, or that our present problems of body stereotyping can be fixed with a better knowledge of it. He said that a clear materialist view of the body as well as its description and context was a significant move in the de-stereotype of the human being. Through knowing the context, he attempts to invoke de-stereotyped produced bodies from contemporary Indian art and politics behind them.

"Women are the weaker sex and need to be protected." "Big boys don't cry." "Women and men are different but equal, and each has a unique role within society." These are only a handful of the sex perspectives that are conveyed in the discourse about women's and men's positions in society. The degree of which all of these views are valid is impossible of deduce, and manifestations of the full spectrum of gender behaviours can be found in society: people who live in their households, remain at home, raise their children and defer to their spouses can be seen in people whose cohabitants live with the children while they go to work. Among them there are a broad variety of different theories to how humans and culture 'shape' or perceive what it is to be one shape from the social connections that individuals have with one another. The arts – Film, video games and literature – express thoughts of what gender-based attitudes look like for children and teens, as well as parents and peers. Studies have demonstrated, for example, that children's books tend to represent girls and boys in a non-stereotypical way; but many libraries and book shops across the globe are still having predated books which contradicts this new representation. Such classic books appear to present children, for example domestic jobs, historically in an acceptable manner, and show children engaging in a broader variety of activities. We often display girls who carry domestic cooking and cleaning objects, while they see boys more often utilizing sporting equipment or producing products.

Charu Gupta has addressed that, this did not stop with women. Some of the films convert the male body and its habits, since they focus on the nude male sex as an advertising culture tool rather than on a feminine one. The display of sexuality among males, particularly through pornographic male songs and dances, gives these ephemeral actions cultural and sexual significance. In famous Bollywood movies and maybe also in our real lives, they pose questions on gender structure. Photos of sexual modesty and nakedness here serve as indicators of market and culture transition, in which the shifting male body is very much engaged in the desire of women. The incarnations of some masculine songs, especially to a degree subvert the conceptions of a patriarchal dominant image, mutate hegemonic manhood and interrogate tidy heteronormative definitions. The spectator's joy and the naked man's appeal seem to be remaining in Bollywood in the coming days.

Deshpande in his article "Indian cinema and the bourgeois nation state" stated that the Indian bourgeois class whose patronage could never be taken for granted by most revolutionaries was a possible source of financing for films. Until independence, the Indian bourgeoisie identify their interests very broadly and waver in response to both colonial and nationalist rule. As proletarian agitation in the 1930s demonstrated, these capitalists rejected films that were dismissive of their party. The army, the Indian bourgeoisie and the major political parties conveniently united against the workers on these class issues. Münshi Premchand's encounter with Mazdoor (worker) reveals how revolutionary cinema has been silenced by corporate interests during his brief trip to Mumbai. The tactical silence of the media is about analphabetism and changes in the education system which promote the market. Mazdoor eventually vanished from the film archives, but it revealed the life and struggle of the Indian working class. The government immediately banned it, on the recommendation of the bourgeoisie of Mumbai, in the midst of growing revolutionary sentiments.

Rao (2010) has pointed out that Bollywood is an Indian film industry, founded in Bombay around 1912. Every year in the studios of the city it makes some 150 Hindi films in the article "The Globalization of Bollywood: An Ethnography of Non-Elite Audiences in India". Well-known for Hollywood's periodic restoration and reorganization, the name acknowledges the Hollywood debt of Bombay's directors as well as a summary of the Hollywood hegemony.

Many are critical of these films and accept the idea that many of them don't represent real India and have commercialism and high earnings as their main goal. We believe we show beauties and rituals that are not actual (Punathambekar, 2005). In comparison, Kapur and Pendakur (2007) supported the unprecedented global demand that India "disappeared" in Hindi cinema as a geographical place. Bombay was a city that was distinct from being an overcrowding, grubby area of the third world, and thus could not be a city under industrial capitalism that was glamourous, affluent or successful (David, 2011). (Punathambekar, A., 2005) in his journal "Bollywood in the Indian-American Diaspora" states that there are still foreigners who have an understanding of the life of India and do not make any mistakes. Basically, they say that they want to watch well-created films with beautiful songs and costumes and do not want to be completely conscious whether they do or don't have positive impact in society.

The dominance of metropolitan and international markets over rural Indian was accomplished by increasing the prices of Hindutva (Indian nationalism) through a right turn in both the political and economic fields. The 1990s saw the latest, more limited country species of popular cinema of Bombay in a country in which 1/3 of the population lives at the edge of poverty. That form removed the questions regarding civil relations, social rights, colonial exploitation, class disputes and labor rules that were there before then to a large degree from the displays. Movies after 1990 became the represented capitalism and exploitation. This is when the women were more oppressed in film industry. India's spectrum and speed flow was increased following progressive and liberal economic initiatives. (Robina Mohammad, 2007) in his article "Phir bhi dil hai Hindustani (Yet the heart remains Indian): Bollywood, the 'homeland' nation-state, and the diaspora" stated that Bollywood took this opportunity in order to meet the challenge of Hollywood and wanted to take advantage of India's buying force. This aimed to become the rising economic force in the film industry in the world. The results were clear in urban India. The world was unexpectedly filled of international brands. Coca Cola McDonald's, Levi's, gives consumers the ability to appreciate the once prerogative of the gourmets. They were reflected by social media, luxurious consumer goods, travel, excursions and global way of life. This paved the way for capitalism in Indian cinema industry. Because, they are the ones who can make a movie happen. So, directors and actors had to compromise their vision.

As stated by (Nimish Adhia, 2013) in his journal "The role of ideological change in India's economic liberalization", it is clear that economists and those who wrote about the causes of economic liberalization in India shared only their views on optimizing capital. Nonetheless, other variables are to be weighed and overlooked. For e.g., a big ideological shift or a society with a completely optimistic improvement in corporate and commercial moral assessment. In this segment we would use the statistics portrayed in popular Hindi films to demonstrate that liberalism before 1980 was replaced by an individualistic mentality, condemning corporate property as an antisocial. These social reforms lead to women getting good roles in media.

Gap of literature

It is difficult to achieve a clear conclusion on the treatment of women and patriarchal law. As women are not a single individual from India and have diverse religions, races, socio-economic class, castes, and ambitions, it can be inferred on Indian silver screens that women are represented on the same basis. The portrait must, of course, react to its genre. Films also must be alert to the sense of the placing of female characters. Women would have an agency, which will replace existing institutional structures and address their own positions within this structure. It is time for the movie to redefine women as artefacts. In addition to myths, the cause of women is significantly assisted in Indian culture. Cinema should have a rare, independent platform for aboriginal people to help them accomplish their wishes. The intention of the film is not love. This will trigger a pursuit of entertainment for social change. In order to express the opinion of people, these should be excluded from all cultural or political ties. In order to facilitate the transition from modernity, films are not to stick to formula movies; they should establish positive images of women. It should make women's representation more inclusive. These depictions recognize women and their role in society.

From the literature survey, it can be seen that the subject of gender subordination and culture hegemony have been studied broadly. The literatures represent the real state of cinema and Indian cinema in general. Though the survey has provided us with lot of insight in to the matter, there are lots more needed to expose the real face on these issues. Also, most of these literatures and the movies mentioned in them are old. A lot of changes have occurred in cinema and society. So, a proper investigation is very much needed to perceive the current situation in the mentioned issues. For this purpose, a new study has been presented in this research based on the presented research methodology.

Chapter Organization

In chapter 2, the literature survey is to be performed on the available papers related to the presented work. In chapter 3, discussion on the factors and various means through which the cinema has its effect on common people on day to day life is presented. The effects and influence of cinema on various levels are detailed here. In chapter 4, the factors responsible for reproduction of culture hegemony are thoroughly explained. The cultural changes and the exposure of certain culture in cinema are briefly discussed. In chapter 5, the analysis and the results are provided. Chapter 6 is constructed so as to provide the overall conclusion on the provided topic.

Conclusion

However, Indian cinema maintains its Indian importance and adheres to Indian values and practices. This is particularly valid as art and life in South Asian culture can hardly be distinguished; they no longer mimic one another, yet appear to blend. The film represents democratic ideologies, moral ideals, collective attitudes, discourses and clothes in culture as well as a commentary on community. In fact, film stars have shifted from their creativity to politics to become powerful personalities who lead the fate of millions. It involves a variety of female actors who acted as the custodian of culture. Such growth demonstrates that not just films but the modern world have been considered to have a female aspect in the entertainment industry. The role portrayed by women in Indian film is a role model for many people who are less willing to participate. With Cinema being a big successful industry, the female characters played in their movies allow Indian women to relate themselves easily with these female characters. The cinema is therefore an essential representation of culture and this interpretation leads to a greater comprehension of community.

Chapter 2
Research Methodology

Introduction

Gender refers generally to the social process of distinguishing individuals and social practices according to sexual identities (Beasley, 2005). It identifies a set of attributes and conducts that women and men expect from society. The definition of gender was introduced to demonstrate the institutional structure of men's and women's interactions and the civil order. By the mid-1980s, men and women's research had moved considerably from the research of women to the study of gender, including examination of how all facets of human life, culture and relationships became sexualised (Kandiyoti, 1996). Lorber (1994) describes gender as a whole social structure, which carries out a system of human desires, directs everyday life processes and is embedded in and an agency in major social institutions such as the economy, philosophy, communities and politics. The sociological viewpoint explores the role of class. The role of gender is the role that society plays between men and women on the basis of their sex. We have an effect on how people view and consider others to be male and female. Such roles are acquired through socialization and defined culturally. Children incorporate social norms and values by studying their social roles and the created outlook of sexual persons (Jackson and Scott, 2002). It's not only about what we are doing, male or female, but also what we do in our sessions. It is created by the relationship and success between individuals.

A critical trend in sociological research is film reflecting social and historical experience in relation to gender approach. The media is critical for constructing gender identities and for socializing gender. Digital culture goods have resources with which we construct our personalities, our selfhood, our religious, racial or nationality structures, our individuality and our 'us and them' (Dines and Humez, 2003). The most prominent social media for engaging with the public are television and film. The idea that film is the mediator of societal reality and personal desires, mutual expectations and ambitions implies that it takes a pioneering aspect as a humanistic discourse with the ability to reorient our daily cultural and material framework (Jain and Rai, 2002).

The role of women in media and women's media are persistent issue in every culture, though patriarchal expectations and women's inequality both represent and reinforce wider gender inequality. In addition, films keep the stereotypical gender stereotypes that women are depicted in culture and society circulating as strongly as they are. Gender and film work addressed the question of the sexuality of women. The study of women's images in films was, in fact, fundamental to the 'second wave' of women's feminism of the sixties and seventies, denouncing women's representations in the entertainment industry and women's positions in entertainment (Jackson and Jacjie in 1998).

In modern India, women's position with the various social movements and a steady change in the understanding of women in society is changed radically. In recent decades women have certainly taken great strides in pursuing equality. In India's social and political system, women played a significant part. India with its rich historical and cultural heritage was a magnificent nation that demonstrates great development in literature. Indian drama and cinema are one of the most common forms of expression. The 1970s saw the emergence of Indian Cinema, a more politically aware and political medium of film, partially funded by public funding, called Parallel Cinema – which is not only part of conventional cinema, but is distinctly distinctive. The image, status and role of women as social issues are represented in India's films and almost from the very beginning were present in popular Indian cinema.

The portrayal of women in film was a significant subject of debate among feminist film theorists in India. The dynamic and fascinating relationship between women and films has significant literary knowledge and some important research on feminism in the Third World that illumines facets of women's inclusion in Indian movies. Women's inclusion and on-screen inclusion are important to an interpretation of women's experiences with the movies in India (Gokulsing and Dissanayake, 1998).

The goal of this study is to examine different styles and patterns of gender representation in Indian films and to understand the public view of women's films. This chapter discusses the study methods, including research architecture, the analysis techniques used and the follow-on testing procedures, as well as goals, description of the framework of the project and strengths of the study. There are also valid reasons for the approaches used to achieve the goal of the analysis.

Objectives of the Study

1. To find out the way in which Indian Cinema influences our everyday life.
2. To find out the parameters responsible for reproduction of culture hegemony.

3. To find out the relationship between cinema and society.
4. To examine the way in which Indian Cinema portray gender, sexuality and their subordination.
5. To find out whether, the discourse and narrative of cinema is reinforcing gender stereotypes and body image ideals.

Research Questions

1. How far the Indian Cinema does influence the everyday life?
2. Does the Indian Cinema help to reproduce the cultural hegemony?
3. How does the culture and society in India respond to the formation of Indian Cinema?
4. To what extent does the Indian Cinema perpetuate the gender inequality or subordination and depict sexuality?
5. Does the Indian Cinema fight out the gender subordination or help to promote the gender exclusion?

Research Methodology

The purpose of this study is to explore different types and trends of cultural hegemony and gender subordination in Indian cinema and society and to find out the perception of the audience regarding gender equality in society and cinema. This chapter discusses the methodology adopted for the study which includes research design, research instruments employed and the research procedures followed. The methods used to meet the objectives of the study are also justified. The study also uses feminist methodology.

Feminist methodology has been developed to address feminist researchers' questions about the boundaries of conventional methodology to capture the perspectives of women and of those excluded in scholarly study. A broad variety of techniques, approaches and analysis tactics are used in feminist methodology. At the start of the 70s, feminist theorists opposed positivist methods of research that limited living conditions to a set of discrete variables which did not satisfy the nuances of social life. Feminists were among the first to emphasize the marginalization of people of color in scholarly study and to suggest research methods against this pattern in academia (Reinharz, 1992).

The importance of intersectional research is highlighted in the study of women's lives by feminist researchers. It highlights the inter-relationships of race, class, sex and gender. The relation between feminist consciousness and women's studies. Over the years, feminist philosophy has established a very broad perspective in study practice, with which a wide variety of subjects can be discussed, men's and women's experiences studied, and local as well as transnational or global structures explored. The intention of those embracing feminist methodologies is to develop awareness for the purposes of social change. Feminist scholars have influenced the style of approach used and the subjects picked for their study. Feminists used participatory action research, for example, to inspire research themes as well as to guarantee that research addresses the demands of individual groups or social movements. This research method is often directed at decreasing the power imbalances between the researcher and the participants.

Research Design

Once the theoretical framework has been established, the next step is to specify the research design to be followed to meet the objectives of the study. Research design is a conceptual framework within which research is conducted. The present study is an exploratory study. In exploratory research, researchers often use qualitative techniques for gathering data and they are less wedded to a specific theory (Gunter, 2002). According to the nature of the objectives of the study, various kinds of the statistical analysis have been used.

In the present study the portrayal of women in society and cinema has been measured from different angles or viewpoints. It aims at finding out the perception of the respondents regarding these portrayals through a survey by the help of the structured questionnaire Data analysis has been done using statistical tools to find out the frequency of the perception of the audience on the basis of their age, education and gender regarding the same.

Universe of the study

The different movies will be selected after 1950 onward (Independent India) and keeping in mind there variety such as art, victorious, romantic, adult etc. These movies will be selected from the internet. As our purpose is to examine the perception of viewers about Indian Cinema and its impact on their lives, so only those people which had keen interest in Indian movies were chose to fill the questionnaire.

Sampling population

The sampling population is defined as the "the population or the universe from which a sample is drawn" (Saunders, Lewis & Thronhill, 2007,). The population for the current study consists of audience of cinema of all types of Indian cinema (Regional Cinema). The respondents were selected from the different categories of viewer (caste, class, occupation, religion, age, areas; rural and urban etc.) as well as this research also have interview of people related to the area of film, media and expert's opinion of the concerning field.

Sampling Techniques

Purposive sampling, specifically systematic purposive sampling is used to have the sample for the study. As our purpose is to examine the perception of viewers about Indian Cinema and its impact on their lives, so only those people which had keen interest in Indian movies were chose to fill the questionnaire.

Data collection Unit

Krippendorff (2004) explains the data collection unit as the recording unit, which is "typically contained in sampling units, at most coinciding with them, but never exceeding them." In this present study the units of data collection are the audience of Indian Cinema which are well aware about the Indian society also. Their responses over the questionnaire are analyzed to meet the objective of the study. In our study the questionnaire was sent to more than 300 people out of whom 256 filled it completely.

Variables Under Study

The following variables are being studied to meet the objectives of the study-

a. General beliefs about society
b. Beliefs about cinema
c. Gender equality
d. Body imaging
e. Decision making
f. Patriarchy in Cinema
g. Change in cinema
h. Impact on everyday life
i. Beliefs about Regional cinema

Reliability of Questionnaire

Reliability is the extent to which an instrument would give the same results if the measurement were to be taken again under the same conditions: its consistency. ***Cronbach's alpha*** is a measure of internal consistency reliability. Most analysis software will also routinely calculate, for each question or questionnaire item in the scale, the value of Cronbach's alpha if that questionnaire item was deleted. These values can be examined to judge whether the reliability of the scale can be improved by removing any of the questionnaire items.

Cronbach's alpha was calculated for the items of the questionnaire. The value of the test statistics was .863 which is greater than .7. It indicates that the questionnaire was highly reliable as a questionnaire is said to be acceptable reliable if its value is greater or equal to .7.

Statistical Tools used for Analysis

In order to examine the impact of gender, age and marital status on the perceptions of people towards society some statistical test were employed. First one was Mann-whitney U test for comparison between two groups and Kruskal- Wallis test for multiple groups.

Mann Whitney U Test

When comparing two independent samples when the outcome is not normally distributed and qualitative, a nonparametric test is appropriate. A popular nonparametric test to compare outcomes between two independent groups is the Mann Whitney U test. The Mann Whitney U test, sometimes called the Mann Whitney Wilcoxon Test or the Wilcoxon Rank Sum Test, is used to test whether two samples are likely to derive from the same population (i.e., that the two populations have the same shape). Some investigators interpret this test as comparing the medians between the two populations. Recall that the parametric test compares the means (H_0: $\mu_1=\mu_2$) between independent groups.

In contrast, the null and two-sided research hypotheses for the *nonparametric test* are stated as follows:

- H_0: The two populations are equal Versus
- H_1: The two populations are not equal.

This test is often performed as a two-sided test and, thus, the research hypothesis indicates that the populations are not equal as opposed to specifying directionality. A one-sided research hypothesis is used if interest lies in detecting a positive or negative shift in one population as compared to the other. The procedure for the test involves pooling the observations from the two samples into one combined sample, keeping track of which sample each observation comes from, and then ranking lowest to highest from 1 to n_1+n_2, respectively.

Kruskal-Wallis Test

The Kruskal-Wallis test is the non-parametric alternative to the One Way ANOVA. *Non parametric* means that the test doesn't assume your data comes from a particular distribution. The H test is used when the assumptions for ANOVA aren't met (like the assumption of normality). It is sometimes called the *one-way ANOVA on ranks*, as the ranks of the data values are used in the test rather than the actual data points.

The test determines whether the medians of two or more groups are different. Like most statistical tests, you calculate a test statistic and compare it to a distribution cut-off point. The test statistic used in this test is called the **H statistic.** The hypotheses for the test are:

- H_0: population medians are equal.
- H_1: population medians are not equal.

The Kruskal-Wallis test will tell you if there is a significant difference between groups.

Significance of the Study

This research demonstrates that the idea of hegemonic femininity has been seen to rise from the dominant women's role over other women's classes. Scholars have pointed out that masculinity is more deeply researched than femininity. Furthermore, most of the research on alternative femininity concentrated on subculture, but this analysis demonstrates that certain types of other femininities are not only embraced by a common subculture. This can be more generally embraced, but should be maintained enough that hegemonic society does not freely oppose this. The research mostly examined the opinions of women in urban environments, skilled residents, and discussed no particular region or culture. This research could contribute to positive improvements in the media environment to make positive film based on reality rather than one sided film.

Limitations the Study has following Primary limitations

- Low availability of data on regional cinema
- Latest data could not be gathered.
- The analysis has its own delimitation due to the financial and time constraints.

Conclusion

The representation of women and patriarchal domination is difficult to reach a consistent conclusion. Given that women are not a single from in India, they are of various faiths, genders, socio-economic status, castes and their interests and aspirations lead to different life situations, it cannot be inferred that women are portrayed on Indian silver screens in an identical way. Naturally, the portrayal must be responsive to their category. For example: The story of a middle-class urban woman would be completely variant from that of a rural female. Movies must also be sensitive to the context in which woman characters are placed. Women will have an organization in place to abolish current institutional systems and to discuss within this system their own roles. It's time for film to redefine women from depicting them as objects. Beyond stereotypes, women's cause in India's society will be greatly assisted. Cinema needs to provide Indian women with a special, autonomous place to assist them fulfill their desires. The object of movie is not to love. This will launch a quest for social transformation through entertainment. This needs to be stripped of any ethnic or political relations to share the opinion of citizens. Film should not adhere to the formula film' as a commodity defined to promote the transition of modernity; it should create more inclusive depictions of women. These depictions will do women credit and their role in society.

Chapter 3
Effect of Cinema in Day to Day Life

Introduction

Cinema Influence the life of everyone and it is also influenced by society at large. Cinema is not limited to merely entertainment rather it demonstrates also social reality and it is strong instrument that affects individuals thinking process.

Cinema is multifaceted in nature; cinema brings with it happiness, sorrow, cultural beliefs, values, violence, and more. It allows to learning the normal as well as abnormal behaviour. A good movie can amuse, teach, and encourage the audience in several respects. Remember, for starters, the influence of music on men. We make us dream. We make us believe. You're leaving us pitiful. We encourage us to support people and to do society well.

At the other side, romantic movies remember why love is necessary and why it should be combated. We help us cry and chuckle at our own emotional shortcomings, so that we can appreciate our friends and families. It's worth living because it helps one feel happy. There are several films whose storylines give us cause to rise and step through the future of joy and hope every morning. We inspire one to overcome emotional suffering and make a meaningful effect on the lives of others. Of starters, films like The Pursuit of Happiness (2006) and The Bucket List (2007) encourage their audiences to try to change the environment for everyone.

Movie also tells all the harmful consequences of drogue, drinking and substance misuse. Crime and violence Tv programs frequently inform viewers about the dangers about abuse, extremism and fighting. Talking of fighting, documentaries allow us to grasp the reality of refugees live and suffering in refugee settlements. Films stimulate solidarity for citizens who have never witnessed civil war in their own right (Smith, 1998). They make us feel guilty, as much as we have never been there ourselves, for our brothers and sisters live in war-torn countries. This is how many voluntary organizations and Trust Funds have raised their visibility.

Every film in a specific culture is planned and created. They embody what we believe in and how we live as individuals. They are an important part of us. It is better than to decode them from our everyday life, to see our worries, personalities, faults and weaknesses in videos. If films test our prevailing values and prejudices, we will doubt ourselves and consider improvement. So, thanks to audiovisual adaptations, people across the world will see films so recognize the lifestyles of remote societies. In addition, that has served to bind us, even though our identities are too different.

The film not only represents our different societies but also shapes our views and ideals for a long time. A clear example is the replication of themes by Hollywood stars and artists. Societies use expression statistics influenced by the entertainment industry are often popular these days. In the very least, the film consolidates and allows certain irrelevant chosen cultural values (Facione, 2011).

Many social psychologists today take the view that films erode people's sympathy by making violence and other people's sufferings acceptable. Temporary apathy is increasing, with many people who choose to passively watch people injure or kill themselves in the bigger urban areas. As a consequence of media desensitizing emotions of concern, the propensity to not support the survivor or tolerate abuse has risen.

Romantic films make sex "sweet" Crime films make deception seem logical. Genres often normalize theft and dishonesty. Teenagers are also allowed to view web pornography videos and stream substance addiction tracks. The entire contents are confusing for young people and women, but parents do not appear to consider secure and foolproof methods to protect their babies.

The cinema has become a powerful tool for, schooling; entertainment and advertising has been powerful cinema. To people around the planet it's a means of relief. This allows one to fight fatigue and removes the frustration and fatigue of the life. This brings you away from all the daily concerns to a world of fantasy (Gabler, 2000). This has the effect of cleaning the mind and strengthening it. Since the beginning of movies, the world of film has always been a rage for the young generation. The young generation, and most often the teenagers, are most affected by the cinema, are followed by it with excitement. This is critical because it is a moment when thousands of ideas and sometimes irrational expectations are about to reach the modern world, and films are playing a vital role in their catering. The threats of the mainstream vulgarity and the derogatory nature of cheap modern movies in pursuit to entertainment are similarly accessible to children and adults. The most powerful and beneficial mass media tool is probably cinema. It can quickly become a form of mass instruction and mass schooling in addition to proving economical entertainment for people. Cinema definitely has a range of strong advantages over other newspapers. It incorporates both audio and video in large part, rendering the human eyes and ears very friendly. It definitely goes beyond the other mediums by progressing color film from the Black and White age of movie making and promoting stereophonic family. The ideals and basic moral principles of the cinema system have a lasting influence on the viewer. The audiences are often linked to the actions and responsibilities of the different characters and personalities through a social, accessible, and long-term consequences of their language and fitness of communication. Maybe the key factor for the creation of a censor board that closely inspects all the scenes that may impact the security of social dignity is the recognition of this aspect. That rule, though, is not relevant nowadays because we are exposed to the Web, in which vulgarity and language are readily accessible to young people as well as to ancient, pornographic and even pornography videos. Here are both the positive and negative effects of film on society:

The Positive Impacts of Cinema on Society

Some films do contain successful, optimistic characters and not all films are bad or unethical. However, it depends basically solely on the film's emphasis and style. Many movies aim to point viewers to various countries' social or political situations. It expands understanding on vices such as condition of women in society, drug abuse, alcoholic beverages, HIV and the diseases of several sexual partners. Cinema seeks to gain an awareness of the value of healthcare, science , art and politics. It also provides us a glimpse into the misery of the weak and the problems of underdeveloped nations and war countries. All these film styles tend to awaken accountability and empathy for these circumstances. Such socially insightful films allow one to grasp the significance of the story. This has a positive impact on our thought and encourages us to bring a contribution to society. In certain instances, after being stirred by a movie, people took up animals and human rights activity (Debjani, 2014).

Figure 3.1: Positive impacts of cinema on society
https://www.google.com/search?q=positive+impact+of+bollywood+on+society

Films held our imagination's improvement. We talk of the things we are looking for and so we move a bit deeper into our creativity and imagine. Even young actors and technicians want to join the film industry because they too discover their creativity and create inspiring content.

Movies is a means of relief, even if the impact is only short-lived for some individuals who wish to forgo worries, tensions and pain. People are amused and focused on issues that have nothing to do with their personal lives.

Positive impacts on youths

Cinema has a beneficial effect on young people as it allows them to interact with people from other cultures. It represents and makes one comfortable with the issues of other societies. In addition, in emergency situations, it also makes people more conscious and helps to improvise.

Progressive ideals like racial equity, selling organs quickly propagate across films. The 'Dangal' series, for example, has encouraged others to support their sports daughters. Today this belief is shifting, and films have a role in this transition too. Lead actors' professions in films profoundly affect young people. While most Indian films concentrate on love between leading characters, several films come these days with beautiful stories and encourage the young to reflect on the aspirations of life rather than only on the love process. Many Indian films are considered to be controversial on contemporary problems and show errors.

The Negative Impacts of Cinema on Society

Films may deliver so well to their market, which is exactly the intention of the advertisement industry. They use video clips for a couple seconds to sell their goods around the globe. For starters, the actors performing their roles show the audience with their latest car model or new designer clothing and accessories. It alerts us, demonstrates curiosity and participation in the latest offering. This helps us to hear about the latest product through the website or through advertising. Therefore, without exhausting the advertisement firms' wallets, the ads and contact loop persisted in smooth travel.

Everything we see and listen to is shaping and manipulating us to a certain extent. We are attempting to mimic and behave like them. We are watching their current developments in design, their chat and their lives on and off television. We want to find out about your work and private life single little bit. That is exactly why it has been banned from smoking in film because viewers watch their beloved stars on the tv and making them believe like they will do it too. We think it's cool because we do so as it gets us back to our favourite stars. In too many different respects, filmmaking has influenced our society. For example, films are primarily responsible for undermining the very foundations of marriage. They make it look like extramarital affairs and polygamous marriages are normal. In actual life, though, it may prove an incredibly dangerous and hazardous activity. Nevertheless, films and their effect on humanity have become very significant and have been part of our very life.

Although films are an excellent source of material, so many movies are detrimental to the heart, eyes and pockets. Furthermore, badly made films may have a rather significant effect on young people's minds. They can lead, by needless violence and obscenity, to various types of crime. The audience may be affected by gazing at so many of these films with a heavy emphasis on aggression and serious subjects.

Figure 3.2: Movie image depicting man's power over women (https://scroll.in/reel/847820/the-list-of-tamil-films-in-which-women-are-destroyed- by-men-is-long-but-it-wasnt-always-that-way)

These cinemas such as shown in Figure 3.1 could badly impact our young generation's moral character if left unchecked. These films should be carefully evaluated by the Censor Board so that the young audience cannot easily view or fully prohibit them.

In brief, films have a tremendous potential both to create a beneficial and detrimental impact on our culture. Therefore, every filmmaker's spiritual duty is to select meaningful stories and to create inspirational films that have a significant effect on society.

Negative Impact on Youths

Indian films are depicting activities such as eve-teaching and harassment as natural and even admirable. This adversely impacts young people and causes them harassers. Many filmmakers neglect their social responsibilities and make their movies prosper by incorporating commercial elements. Those filmmakers produce films which do not provide society with something positive, but which propagate negative factors such as crime, staying, etc. Indian films nowadays target women by the inclusion of products or unique songs. Interestingly, they advocate the importance of gender on the one side and create songs that are demeaning for women on the other. Male plum consume alcohol and prove that it is admirable in the majority of Indian films. Male cigarettes also feature in several films as shown in Figure 3.2.

Figure 3.3: Protagonist smoking in the movie Kabir Singh (https://www.ndtv.com/entertainment/kabir-singh-shahid-kapoor-explains-smoking- and-drinking-scenes-in-film-2037065)

It concerns young adults with intense feelings. Films are often comfort, yet never reveal medium-sized lives. It raises consumerist culture which would have the greatest effects on young people. Several filmmakers force their beliefs on culture through films. This kind of film can negatively represent other cultures or faiths. Films encourage vengeance for men. Few films demonstrate the main protagonists fail lawfully. Most films destroy villains themselves with main actors. This affects our culture and our law enforcement.

There are so many work has been done in the area of negative impact of cinema and so on. In early 1972, a series of conducted research that revealed the origin of the children's exposure to television aggression and their resulting violent actions had, for the first time, been gathered by Surgeon General's Office of the United States National Institutes of Health. This implied that violence on TV or in film might inspire certain children or encourage them to engage in actions of abuse or crime.

The latest established trend named "global apathy" is a point of anxiety for many social scientists that are prepared to stand by as others are hurt or murdered, and the investigators can do little to support victims. It means that humans respond unfeelingly or indifferently to the misery of other individuals.

A reason for this apathy is that certain people have become desensitized to the violence that happens predominantly in the media, especially in greater metropolitan areas. Although there is a large amount of violence in media and film in the United States, that is an issue and concern for other technologically developed nations around the world where a strong proportion of the populace is fitted with a TV screen.

Psychiatrist Fredric Wertham remarks "Through TV and moving pictures a child may see more violence in thirty minutes than the average adult experiences in a lifetime. What children see on the screen is violence as an almost casual commonplace of daily living. Violence becomes the fundamental principle of society, the natural law of humanity. Killing is as common as taking a walk, a gun more natural than an umbrella. Children learn to take pride in force and violence and to feel ashamed of ordinary sympathy. They are encouraged to forget that people have feelings."

The dissertation of a researcher from Stanford University, Albert Bandura, in the area of simulation and mimic learning shows a second big problem alongside the desensitization of emotional emotions. He and a variety of colleagues have collected a great deal of data in recent years that has demonstrated consistently and forcefully how live shows may teach new models of opinions and affect or even alter beliefs, behaviours and principles or those on the TV and theater screen.

Recent research shows that media and film are important vehicles for demonstrating good and bad. Movies appear to have a great potential to warn, teach, inspire and at times even alter actions, yet there is little question. The basic idea behind modeling and imitation learning is that if you want someone to follow a new practice, you expose someone who shows it in glamorous and desirable situations live or televised.

The role of TV and films, which may lead to antisocial breakdowns and societal disorder, in promoting abuse, transmitting ideals and influencing a range of life patterns, definitely underlies inquiry.

The interpretation of the problem as basic "impact" that a movie picture has is inappropriate as it means that, like triggers, films have such impacts on audience that are more or less inert or especially spectacular in any way and may thus be affected or manipulated in a specific direction. The one-way architecture of results is commonly accepted. Many people were fascinated by the perceived passivity of the movie viewers which established the foundation for certain perceptions and opinions about the presumed positive and negative impacts of films. A stronger explanation of our question will be: what is the impact on the viewer of the quality of movies? Quite specifically, what do viewers get out of the movies they watch and why?

The problem as to the trigger interest of the motion picture is posed in these words. It's the universal ideals that films convey and to the degree films transmit these principles in our culture. To grasp this incredibly complicated mechanism involving speech and contact, much must be understood of the nature of this project, the psychological needs of its exposed individuals, the local climate, and the social and cultural powers that act on filmmakers (Srinivas, 2002).

We have very little to tell about any of these issues given the way we have been studied. It is surprising that a company that has embraced the fifth-largest position in the United States has performed very little rigorous work on the substance or its acceptability criteria. This is clear that most clichés tend primarily to reflect the positive reactions of films of people in and beyond the company. There are also clichés. For starters, such a perception is sometimes articulated that films offer a way of avoiding the nature of life as "pure entertainment. Any criticism by other individuals outside the sector may have the impact that movies have real and possible adverse impacts on the public, far from being "mere" entertainment. Of these purposes, Entertainment is the symbol of evil, and the output is so likely to be spiritually debauching that endless security forces are considered to be essential or too full of political propaganda.

Curiously complex and sometimes conflicting are the theoretical views towards the issue of the results of how movies influence human behaviour, as we have recast the question. These are focused on a variety of observations about human behaviour and the response about human animals in social circumstances. Since these attitudes are also the reference frames for considering the position of the motion picture in our society both by the layman and by the expert, it may be helpful, to summarize such attitudes.

Research Analysis

Indian media are obviously facing many obstacles as they work to protect freedom of speech, find ways to express themselves, seek to report on and alter dynamic social reality or even make a decent living. Women and men will work together for these ideals and for justice in the workplace and in the wider community. Research was conducted and statistics from secondary data sources consisting of magazines, books, newspapers, and websites as well as Indian cinema from 2010 to 2015 were collected for data.

Table 3.1: Image of women in printed media

S. No.	Image of women (Categories)	Number of women image in print media	
		N	%
1.	Domesticated/take care of house	30	20.0
2.	Business women/career women	15	10.0
3.	Fashionable/stylish & glamorous/decorative	32	21.33
4.	Emancipated women	14	9.33
6.	As sex object/exposer of female body	47	31.33

Source:https://www.google.com/search?q=Image+of+women+in+printed+media

Above the table shows that the majority of print media, such as books , magazines , newspapers, periodicals and website, that portray and advertise women as sex objects and exhibitors (31.33%), then trendy and glamorous (21%) women, then domesticated (approximately 20%). Positive inclusion of women less centered on working women or business women (20%), women who are emancipated (9.33%) and women in education (8 percent). This representation also indicates that the pretty image is not in the interest of such print media. It's a really fast business world but that doesn't mean they can get to the top by losing their integrity and honor, and selling their body as an item. Each time the emphasis is on women's optimistic and solid role in understanding and accepting democratic cultures.

Table 3.2: Image of women in visual media

S.No.	Role play	Numbers of role played by actress in top 10 hit movies(60) of year 2010-2015	
		N	%
1	Dependent Mother/ Wife house wife	18	30
2	Arrange Marriage and parenthood	20	33.33
3	Supports male protagonist to achieve his goal	6	10
4	Girlfriend/ lover	35	58.33
5	Career goal oriented	5	8.33
6	Emancipated women/ empower women/daring	7	11.66
7	Dancer (Night club/bar/cabaret)/ exposer of female body	26	43.33
8	Prostitute/call girl / courtesan	4	6.66
9	Home maker (Takes care of children, Takes care of 10- laws)	30	50
10	More passive than men/ less intellectual/rebellious	9	15

Source:https://www.google.com/search?q=Image+of+women+in+printed+media

The table above reveals that most of the films depict women as wives or as partners (around 58%) and then home building artists (50%), who devote all of their time on caring for families, children and lawyers. Afterwards, the women are represented as a dancer in the night club, dance bar / cabaret and expose the men's bodies for sex. This demonstrates that in order to warm the public's eyes women are being repressed as a sex object. Characters like prostitute / mobile / cortesian are somewhat limited in many ways as if to equate old films (before many decades). Women continue to view their son and husband as vulnerable mother / wife / housewife. Females still have less accountability for showing parenthood. Data also show that, although we are still scientists and modern women, they are not emancipated and independent, although they are advanced and fully educated, to consider choosing a life partner.

Males are reported an average of 30% in the Wikipedia plot over the nearly 50 years compared to women who are only stated 15 times in the cast category. According to the researchers, the task of an actress is not as critical as that of the actor.

Adjective description of men and women in Indian cinema are shown in Figure 3.3. The characters in women often are identified as "strong" and "successful" associated with surface-level qualities, desirable and beautiful. "...verbs like 'kills' and 'shoots' occur with males while verbs like 'marries' and 'loves' are associated with females," the researchers noted. Women are much happier and less angry than people in previews. In line with studies dating from 2012, commercial Hindi movies have found that "ideal women" are submitted, self-sacrificed, chaste and regulated, while the "bad" woman is "individualistic, sexually aggressive, westernized, and not sacrificing."

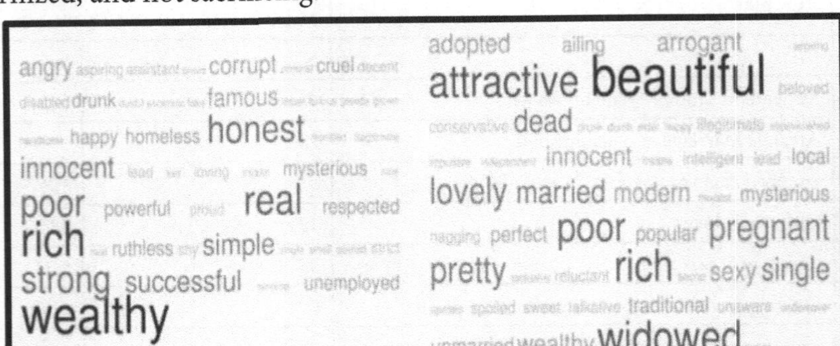

Figure 3.4: Adjective description of men and women in Indian cinema (https://themitpost.com/women-indian-cinema-tale-representation/)

The data also show that descriptors for males are profession-driven during introductory sequences, while females have a so-called 'wife of' or 'the daughter of' association with physical appearances, emotional statements or their relationship to the male. In most stories, men had higher occupations: more than 32% of men were physicians, as opposed to only 3% of women; for women, teachers and secretaries were the most common professions. Male characters performed predominantly the parts of prosecutors, Businessmen and police officers.

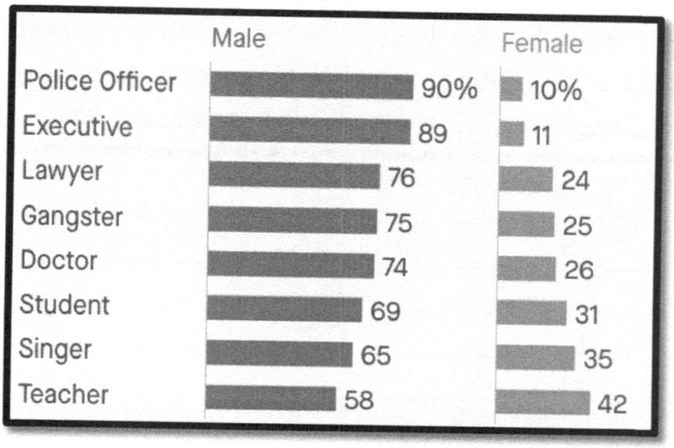

Figure 3.5: The roles of men and women in Indian cinema (Madan et al., 2017)

The profession played by both men and women in Indian cinema is shown in Figure 3.4. Although their role is trivialized, moviemakers are not reluctant to use women as the bait for theatre-filled audiences. Although 80% of films have mentions of husbands rather than women, remarkably more than 50% of film posters have actresses. The studies have identified that in the films, the men have more than 100 references in the story and the women do have none. Nishtha Madaan said of IBM India, that they would like to make it public (the actress), but she's sidelined when it comes to actual story. Sameep Mehta from IBM and the Indraprastha Informatics Institute, Delhi and the Technical University of Delhi, have co-written Madaan's paper.

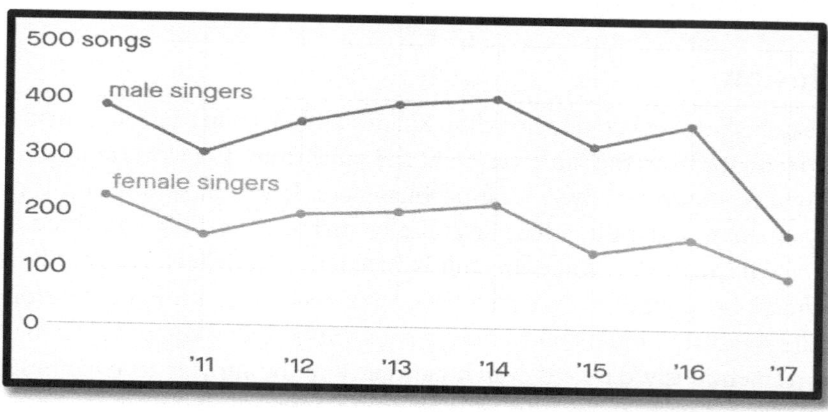

Figure 3.6: Number of singers of both genders utilized in soundtrack (Madan et al., 2017)

In the meantime, women other than actresses are not being given any attention. Since 2010 a soundtrack study of the movies reveals that women consistently sing less than male a pattern leading women vocalists addressed. If the true portion of the soundtrack is taken into consideration, this trend is even more dreadful, the researchers say.

From the graph, it can be clearly seen that the number of female singers is very low when compared with number of male singers. In fields such as production, direction and cinematography, women are also mostly absent.

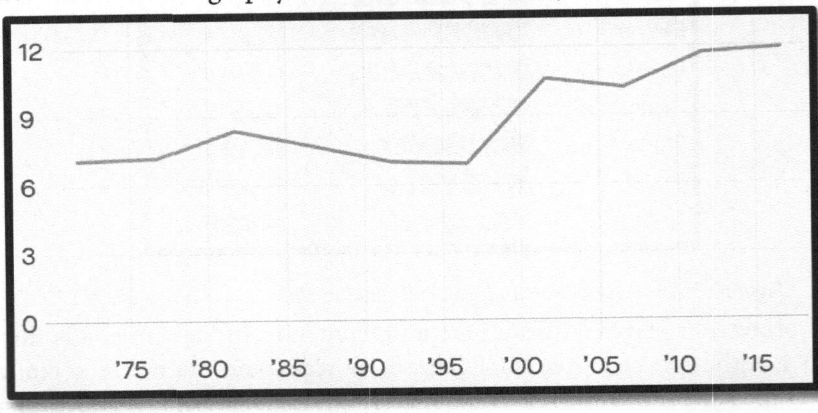

Figure 3.7: Women centric movies released in four decades (Madan et.al.,2017)

While this stereotype represents the 'how people think,' it also represents the 'how men think.' In recent years, the proportion of female-centered films has grown. "In the last three years, it has been found at least 30 films where females play an important role in both the plot and the poster," the study stated. In 11.9 percent of Hindi films released from 2015 to 2017, females were the key characters. In the 1970s, the number was lower than 7%.

Conclusion

The research shows effectively how film shapes and develops societal norms while seeking feedback from the same viewer at the same time. The views and beliefs that people make on our society's social problems are driven in significant, if not full ways by cinema. Some films have eventually stirred the public and lifted a hand against social inequality. There are still behaviours and beliefs of our culture that are founded on prejudice and that have preserved our country's development. Caste rule rigidity, untouchability, dowry rule and purdah structure have made our culture tremendously damage. Much can be done by movies to end these evils. Cinema may be used to encourage national integration, banishment, weddings, family planning, eradication of analphabetism and so forth. These issues will encourage our culture to improve. The cinema can be used as an instrument to support and guide the people along the right road to get rid of obscurantism. This will help eradicate our society's prejudice. Not only this, it can introduce and implement several much-needed social reforms using the cinema.

Chapter 4
Media, State and Society

Introduction

This chapter is an attempt to sketch the relationship among the media (media in general Cinema in particular), state and society. State is creating regulatory bodies for the controlling of agencies like media. Governing of the society is the sole responsibility of state. There are plenty of theories who describes how state control the society e.g. Karl marx, Louis Althusser, Antonio Gramsci so on. State is always vocal towards the power, influence, Sovereignty, war, control, national power. It is compatible with patriarchy as socialist feminism claims. It is well observed idea that both state and patriarchy creating space for capitalism and male domination. There is very few examples of women who secure political position in higher level, in our country we have only once a women prime minister.

Media work under the control of state and sponsored by capitalist class while the nexus between state and capitalist well established fact in contemporary era. Indian cinema not challenge the ideology rather focused on economic gain. Such condition is come to the society through the filtration of media. The nature of state is controlling over the population given to the specific territory. This is become the part of exisiting culture. Such idea is confirmed by the eminent scholar like Karl marx, Louis Althusser, Antonio Gramsci and this idea is extended toward patriarchy in the contribution of R.W.Connell in her concept hegemonic masculinity. She try to combine Gramsci hegemony in the discourse of feminism and create a relationship between hegemony and masculinity or finding the answer of the question The place of women in power position.

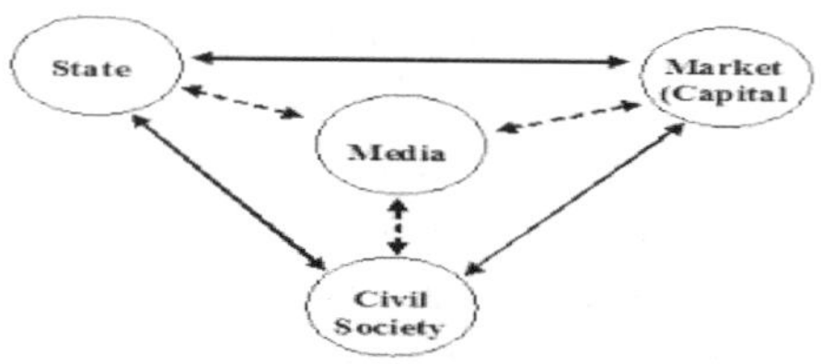

Figure 4.1: Relation between media, state and society (https://www.google.com/search?q=media+state+and+society)

It clearly seems in above figure 4.1 that media is center in society and all three affects each other. But the state that I have mentioned above, support capitalism tries to control the media.

State use media as an instrument to maintain or perpetuate power structure of capitalist class.

Capitalist class always tries to show only those things which are helpful in maintaining their dominance.

Media through Social Thinkers

Perhaps beginning with Frankfurt's theoretical study of the "culture industry", specifically Max Horkheimer, Theodor W. Adorno and Herbert Marcuse's research, theoreticians tried to understand the effect that mainstream audiences are having on and can have an impact on the vast media system. Reflecting this, Adorno and Horkheimer stated:

"The most intimate reactions of human beings have been so thoroughly reified that the idea of anything specific to themselves now persists only as an utterly abstract notion: personality scarcely signifies anything more than shining white teeth and freedom from body odor and emotions. The triumph of advertising in the culture industry is that consumers feel compelled to buy and use its products even though they see through them." (Horkheimer et.al., 1972, p.167). Early theoreticians like this saw no organization representing the entertainment industry public at all, arguing instead that the market was focused on collective deception action and that the ordinary customers were a moral repetition, inculcating without understanding the ideals of the dominant classes. It was a reinstatement, by many opponents of this school, of Marx's proposals for manipulation or media as proponents of a dominant philosophy, which was dismissive of the prospect of mainstream media consumers acting against these prevailing ideas.

Publicity includes a picture about a specific way of life and different strata of society. "The life styles of upper-class are mostly portrayed in the entertainment contents to create a sense of desire and aspiration amongst the viewing public towards such life styles" (Roy, 2012). Advertising played a significant part in the creation and dissemination of ideas in the public sphere. "Advertisements would ….act as ideological apparatuses" (Chaudhuri, 2001). The hegemony of the dominant classes continues ideological manipulation in a free society. Gramsci presented the theory of hegemony in his Prison Note Books. The ruling bourgeoisie uses the process by which the dependent classes receive their approval. The ideas governing society are presented in such a way that they appear as ideas for society as a whole. "The world view of the ruling class, in other words, was so thoroughly diffused by its intellectuals as to become the common sense of the whole of society" (McLellan, 2008). The ruling majority takes refuge under the aegis of hegemony in order to obtain general consent to their domination. Dominant ideology becomes invisible because it is translated into common sense, appearing as the natural, apolitical state of things (Chaudhuri, 2001).

One can argue that the ongoing proliferation of the mass media, civil society and their thinkers is the justification for the continued survival of the dominant ideas. They thus represent their interests as the interests of the public as a whole. Noam Chomsky, an anarchist and radical US academic manipulation model for mass media exploitation, offering support and perpetuating the capitalist class supremacy. The dominant culture is nurtured and covered by advertising and showing news and opinions. "This distortion operates through series of filters, such as the impact of private ownership of media outlets, a sensitivity to the views and concern of advertisers and sponsors and the sourcing of news and information from agents of power such as governments and business think tanks" (Heywood, 2004). This is the politics of dominance or wealth that targets us in numerous speeches for a dictatorship. A dominant stratum of society is still looking for a method to control the regulation. Throughout that purpose, it creates its own dialogue and uses different methods throughout to integrate it into the general public. "Society......requires discourse the mapping, description and articulation of situations and processes) which by definition has the effect of annihilating and delegitimizing certain views and positions while including others" (Van, 1994).

In brief, the dominant discourse, for fear of losing their rights and reputation, purposely avoids or subverting the remainder of the discourse. Thanks to their failure to propagate through civil society and the general population, other expressions are subjugated. A modern middle-class norm is being applied to the ads. There is a deliberate effort to encourage and re-establish a new Indian regulatory market. Such advertising quietly but essentially rule out the picture of another world which contains poor, tribal, labor, farmers and Dalit. Although there has been a glaciation in India's economy in the 1990s; neo-liberal economic neutralization of cultural distinctions is argued for and encourages total democracy in which inequality in no form is encouraged, social value is guiding factor. Economic structures and taboos are going to vanish. The celebration of freedom and liberation will happen when the modern India has absolute independence.

In reality, however, there is a modern method of culture and norm. The modern Indian is conceived as an educated, upper caste, cosmopolitan, scientifically conscious rationalist with respect to agricultural, an alphabets or semi-literate mindset, a lower case, a parochial mind. The new person was designed as "....the typical corporate executive, an upwardly mobile professional who travels a great deal, works hard, and unwinds at weekends and holidays" (Chaudhuri, 2001). Regarding Indian women, the same is applicable. In the nationalist rhetoric that represented women "educated, politically conscious and somehow innocent in Western cultural mores," previous pictures of Indian women were taken. This portrayal is endorsed on Indian women by a traditional nationalism that portrays women as chaste, demure, and physically pure. The other female is without education, cultural and moral tags and politeness. This image of 'other woman' is magnificently depicted by Partha Chatterjee. "who was coarse, vulgar, loud, quarrelsome, devoid of superior moral sense, sexually promiscuous, subjected to brutal physical oppression by males" he labels them common women (Chatterjee, 1989). This female is socially less recognized and less respected. "Alongside the parody of the westernized woman, this other construct is repeatedly emphasized in the literature of the nineteenth century through a host of lower-class female characters who make their appearance in the social milieu of the new middle class—-maid servants, washer women, barbers, peddlers, procuresses, prostitutes" (Chatterjee, 1989). Throughout post-independent India, the common woman or the other woman developed a great expectation that this partiality would be abolished. To order to resolve social obstacles and impediments, Indian Constitutions Fathers initiated the ideals of democracy, equity, fairness, the elimination of untouchability with the goal of increasing unity and eliminating prejudice and injustice from everywhere. "Written into the Indian constitution was a pledge to battle against discrimination on grounds of sex, caste, community, class and tribe" (Chaudhuri, 2001). The state of the other woman remains essentially the same after several years of freedom. Their goal circumstances are not motivated by the scale of growth and modernization.

State control of Media

The reality that media discourse is an atmosphere of near-interaction between creators and viewers presumably applies to people's participation in an interactive world that functions by manipulating the knowledge required for people's minds to be shared. The manipulator, which is particularly labelled as the state, exercises this mental power by amusing discourses and other interactions. The state, the official authority, is largely dependent on such a control source, as Lippmann called the "the bewildered herd". This power, however, took various forms and created numerous means of controlling the entity. In reality, in every culture the key goal of the media is "restrict the public arena and transfer decisions to the hands of uncountable private tyrannies" in which the "removing the public from potential influence on policy" (Chomsky, 2007) plays a significant part. In other words, people should stay outside political space and essentially avoid entering into the affairs of the elites.

In 'sham democracy' people are gentle civilians who engage in what the government offers them, scream political slogans and accept what is shared in the Cinema. The advertising in the media depends on some templates to convince a broader variety of people to sell their goods. In other words, citizens and masses continue to be the main objectives of this propaganda which attempts to unify the conviction of common and reasonable things. This is done by building the illusion of ideal society, which cannot exist without the normal way of life projected on the system's screens.

In reality, cinema excel in propaganda by portraying a collection of principles as the only workable one. A greater degree of engagement with the actors and behaviour on the screen than seen anywhere in mainstream culture. These values will represent social norms as well as form them over a period of years (O'Donnell and Garth, 1992).

The media, as an agent of social conditioning, may be seen as a tool to expose the injustice to general crowds by the ruling body (e.g. the dominant and the hegemonic male order). According to Chafetz (1997), that inequality is intertwined in capitalist structures like the work force. The household and the work force benefit working class men, since females provide domestic service and hence are designated for men to better pay jobs. The low pay or lack of work prospects cause women to rely on their spouses and make them the domestic worker, who often decrease their workplace salaries to a subordinate position (Chafetz, 1997). Chaftez says,

> *"an ideology of patriarchy, or male supremacy, fostered by capitalists, undergirds and sustains both forms of female oppression. This ideology justifies women's non-waged domestic responsibilities with reference to biologically rooted reproductive differences between men and women and justifies gender-based labor market inequities with reference to women's domestic obligations." (p. 105)*

Media have so many effects on culture or society. It is the media for the masses that enable them to understand a great deal and to shape opinions and judge different matters. It is the media that brings people up to date with the news and the environment we all learn meaning from it. The media influences the outlook of people. So much media interference is an issue of concern about all. Media can be seen as the political democracy's "watchdog."

The main aim of the media, particularly cinema is to ideologically dominate the minds of the masses. Media embraces philosophies that encourage globalization, privatization, colonialism, sectarianism, misogyny, militarism, oppressive violence, vigilance and antagonism toward working people. The reality does not depend on transparency in mainstream media, but on repetition. When an assumption is repeated more than three times a concept becomes a reality.

What drives this influential tool to propagate and to accept? Money is the bottom line. Film industry aim to achieve revenues from revenue from the box office. TV studios make profits by recruiting huge numbers of citizens. This is one of the reasons that sex and violence have such an important role to play in cinemas. Selling gender and violence, drawing crowds means money.

Power is one of the sources of disparity between men and women. Gendered media contents illustrate gender dynamics, since television is a collective entity, has a huge influence on television listeners. An improved social structure represents political and economic expectations of governing society.

> *"Media content is both a manifestation and a source of culture. That is, media content takes elements of culture, magnifies them, frames them, and feeds them back to an audience. Media impose their own logic in creating a symbolic environment. If we assume that culture must change, adapt, and improve, then media content may serve as either a catalyst for or a brake on this change." (Shoemaker & Reese, 1996, p. 60)*

The control of a culturally complex society by the dominant class in the Marxist ideology means that the culture of that society — the views and explanations, attitudes, traditions and values— can be converted into agreed societal norms by forced and ruling classes. The uniformly applicable prevailing philosophies, as well as artificial social systems serving only the governing class, which excuse the status quo of the religious, political and economic ones as normal and inevitable, perpetual and advantageous to every social class. The Italian philosopher and politician Antonio Gramsci originally developed this Marxist study, which explores how the dominant capitalist class (the bourgeoisie) develops and retains power. The structuralism philosopher Louis Althusser proposed the idea of the intellectual system of the state as the philosophical critic to cultural hegemony, to explain the process of dynamic interactions between various State structures, through which ideology is translated and distributed to society's populations.

Gramsci analyses the social terrain under which 'leadership' is disputed with the definition of 'apparato egemonico' or 'apparato di egemonia.' The definition seeks to examine certain modes and aspects of oppression or the acquisition of control by the underprivileged groups, which are based on consensus. Any organization, position or agent organizing, mediating and establishing class superiority over other groups can be described as a hegemonic apparatus. Gramsci explains his 'philosophy of praxis' as a mission to overcome such subordination. The implementation, in the sense that it "creates a new intellectual terrain, is like the transformation of consciously and knowledge. The implementation of a hegemonic apparatus leads to a 'philosophical reform.'

Gramsci's conceptions of power "nuanced" is that power primarily existed within the sphere of "hegemonic" discourse, on the basis of reciprocal relations between the economy and politics. (Jones, 2006). The concept of control of Gramsci is incorporated into "force relations." The dynamic nature of control within society remains in power. It is there and it can be observed. The ruling bourgeois class primarily exercises its influence by means of ideology: through the institutions of civil society it acts on the common mindset by maintaining hegemony utilizing the state apparatus. Strength, theory, and action-philosophy (praxis) were inseparable from Gramsci's conception.

> *"...a social group may have its conception of the world...but this same group has for reasons of submission and intellectual subordination, adopted a conception which is not its own and it affirms this conception verbally and believes itself to be following it, because this is the conception which follows in normal times... This is when the conduct is not independent and autonomous, but submissive and subordinate." (Gramsci, 327).*

Gramsci defines the State as "the entire complex of practical and theoretical activities with which the ruling class not only justifies and maintains it dominance, but manages to win the active consent of those over whom its rules" (Carnoy 1986, 65).

In cinema, one can experience the connection between all these entities. As the culture is open to changes, it can be changed by whoever is in the power by manipulating people's mind by spreading propaganda through cinema as the culture hegemony is very hard to identify. Even without their own knowledge, people tend to follow whatever they are shown in the cinema. When the state decides to spread a particular propaganda, they tend to make use of the cultural references in cinema. And many of the cultures have subordinated gender on various conditions. So, when they try to show this in cinema, they had to subordinate one gender or other so as to favor their propaganda.

Another source of cinema and television's success is that audiences search for items that offer instant benefits – exciting pleasure and hyperreality. In the field of semiotics and postmodernism, hyper reality is an unwillingness of knowledge, in particular in technologically sophisticated postmodern cultures, to differentiate between illusion and reality. A French sociologist Jean Baudrillard concocts the postmodern semiotic idea of "hyperreality." Hyperreality is seen as a state in which reality and fantasy are effortlessly merged, so that no reasonable difference remains between the end of one end and the beginning of another. It allows physical reality to be mixed with augmented reality and human comprehension with artificial intelligence. For various factors, people may be more attuned or interested in the hyperreal universe and not so much in the actual real world. As a framework for understanding current cultural conditions, especially in cinema, Hyperreality is important. Hyperreality in our society is a threat; people will observe and embrace hyperreal representations as representations because the representations do not actually reflect true physical individuals. This can lead to a search for an unrealistic ideal or a lack of unimpaired role models.

An element that affects the content of contemporary cinemas is the personal agendas of creators and producers from elite culture who desire to reshape society along the lines of their desires. The elite culture is the group whose members are in the lead or who hold more power than other classes. The elite cultured people strive to dominate others by having their culture as reference culture for the rest of the community. The cultural hegemony is thus passed on through the cinemas. The last few decades show the devastating effects of this effort to use mass media to reform society.

Today, Indian cinema is no longer afraid of choosing sides. Besides the film on Modi, a series of political biopics such as "Thackeray" and "The Accidental Prime Minister" have been released in various languages. Though "Thackeray" lionized Bal Thackeray, the father of Shiv Sena, BJP 's coalition ally in Maharashtra, "The Accidental Prime Minister" ridiculed and vilified Manmohan Singh, the Gandhis and other members of the Congress party.

Conclusion

Media may not only have a main role to play in society. In matters such as culture creation, "regionalism," the development of a democratic community they influence values, views and areas of concern too. Cinema has a specific duty, particularly in developed countries with as much poverty and misgovernment as India. Indian society press has a duty that is closely related to the socio-economic circumstances. Cinema has a particular responsibility. The current scenario is not very reassuring and certain areas must be tackled. The self-regulatory system in all media organizations, when it occurs, needs to be strong enough to prevent anomalies. Agencies such as the Indian Press Council should be careful to stop the root. The media is therefore responsible for the accuracy and accountability of information to readers, viewers and listeners. Furthermore, mostly the media has been incorporating a key feature of our era and it is politics, law, or other social issues that influence every citizen.

Chapter 5
Cinemas Today: Experiences from the Field

Introduction

This chapter deals with the data of responses collected from the viewers of Indian cinema. In order to examine what are the beliefs of Indian cinema audience about the reproduction of cultural hegemony and gender subordination a survey was conducted in which audience of Indian cinema participated voluntarily. A structured questionnaire was prepared keeping in mind the objective of the study. The questionnaire was shared with the participants through digital platforms like mail, WhatsApp etc. They filled it with their own thinking process without any external biasedness. A total of 256 participants filled the survey form. This chapter explains the trends of thinking process of the respondents about the Indian culture and the Indian cinema. The frequency distributions of the Reponses will show what do the Indian cinema viewers feels about the effect of cinema everyday life and how it affects the cultural beliefs of the people.

Demographic Profile of Respondents

Table 5.1: Demographics of Respondents

Gender	**Frequency**	**Percentage**
Female	139	54. 3
Male	117	45.7
Total	256	100.0
Marital status		
Unmarried	59	23.0
Married	197	77.0
Total	256	100.0
Education		
Higher	243	94.9

Secondary	13	5.1
Total	256	100.0
Income		
Average	121	47.3
Higher than average	28	10.9
Lower than average	37	14.5
Much higher than average	1	.4
Much lower than average	69	27.0
Total	256	100.0

The above table indicates the demographic profile of the respondents. Out of 256 respondents 54.3 % were females and 45.7% were males. 77% of the respondents were married and 33% were unmarried.94.9% of the respondents had higher education and 5.1% had secondary education.47 of the respondents had average income, 10.9% had higher than average income,14.5% had lower than average income,.4 had much higher than average income,27% had much lower than average income.

General beliefs about Indian Culture and Gender Subordination

Before focusing on cinema, it is very important to know how people think about their own culture and what they think about the gender subordination in their society. It is necessary to examine that how the gender are being treated in the society so that it could be seen whether the content shown in Indian cinema is actual picture of what happening in society or it is prompting gender subordination Indian cinema.

Table 5.2: Frequency distribution of the responses about Indian culture and gender subordination

Statements	Frequency	Percentage
Do you think that Indian society all genders are treated equally?		
No	220	85.9
Yes	36	14.1
Total	256	100
Do you think that women are dominated by men in Indian Society?		
No	51	19.9
Yes	204	80.1

Total	255	99.6
Do you think that women have equal right to take decision in Indian society?		
No	164	64.1
Yes	92	35.9
Total	256	100.0
Do you think in Indian society women has equal rights of education and to make a career choice (this is not about legal right - it is about social right?		
No	139	54.3
Yes	117	45.7
Total	256	100.0
Indian culture worships goddess, do you think on ground women have the same level respect?		
No	200	78.1
Yes	56	21.9
Total	256	100.0
Do you think in Indian in spite of being educated women are forced to be more oriented towards taking care of home and children?		
No	35	13.7
Yes	221	86.3
Total	256	100.0

The above table represents the frequency distribution of the responses collected about the general beliefs of the audience of Indian cinema. They were if all the genders are treated equally in the society, 85.9% of them responded that all genders are not treated equally in the society. Which shows that a huge proportion of the people believes that all genders are not treated equally. When they were asked if the women is dominated by men in Indian society, 80.1% of the respondents answered in yes, which indicates that women is highly dominated by men in our society. The respondents were asked if the women have equal right to take decision, 65% of the respondents answered that no women do not have equal right of decision making in the society, which means a very low proportion of women has equal right to take decisions. The respondents were asked if Indian society provides women equal rights of education and to make a career choice, on that 45.4 % of the respondents said yes and rest 54.6% said no, which means that out of 256 respondents nearly half thinks that women have equal right to education and choosing career and more than half thinks they do not. it shows that they cannot even take decision for their own career. In Indian culture and religions women is worshiped is as goddess for a long time, there are many goddesses which are believed to be source of energy and power. The respondents were asked if on the ground level women is treated with that respect which people give to the goddess the results show that 78.1% of the respondents thinks that factually women do not have that kind of respect in Indian society. It means that people worship goddess but real women is believed to be weak.86.3% of the respondents agreed that no matter how educated or successful a woman is in field of her career, she is always forced to be oriented towards taking care of home and her children.

The analysis of the perceptions of people towards gender equality and culture shows that all genders are not equally treated in Indian society. Women is dominated by men and supposed to be weaker, depending on men and they do not have freedom to make decisions.

Beliefs about Indian Cinema

Cultural Hegemony in Indian Cinema

It was supposed that the Indian cinema is affecting the cultural beliefs and is affecting the cultural beliefs and affecting the mindsets of people about their culture. In order to know what is the perception of the audience of Indian cinema on the point some questions were asked to them about the effects of the movies. Following are the results obtained from the survey-

Table 5.3: Perceptions about Cultural hegemony in Indian cinema

Statements	Frequency	Percentage
Do you think that Indian cinema is working in direction to show that foreign culture is much better than Indian culture?		
No	74	28.9
Yes	181	71.1
Total	256	100
Do you think that the Indian cinema gives a negative mark of Indian culture on viewers mind?		
No	100	39.5
Yes	155	60.5

Total	255	100
Do you think that Indian cinema is manipulating the cultural beliefs of the audience specially the youth?		
No	57	22.3
Yes	199	77.7
Total	256	100.0
Do you think that Indian cinema shows men having more potential than real situation (like fighting with multiple people single handed and defeating them)?		
No	37	14.5
Yes	219	85.5
Total	256	100.0

The respondents were asked if Indian cinema is trying to show that foreign culture is much better than Indian culture, 71.1% of the respondents believes that cinema is showing foreign culture is good while degrading the Indian culture. A huge proportion of respondents believing that indicates cinema is actually working in that direction from audience point of view. The respondents were asked if Indian cinema frames a negative shape of Indian culture in mind of audience, 60 % of the respondents found to believe in the same. Which means most of the respondents thinks Indian cinema is showing us a negative picture of Indian culture. The respondents were asked if Indian cinema is trying to manipulate the cultural beliefs of people, especially the youth, 77.7% of the participants shown agreement to that statement. It shows that Indian cinema is actually manipulating the youth about their cultural beliefs by showing the comparison between different religions and cultures. After that they were asked if cinema shows men over powerful like fighting with multiple people single handed, 85% respondents agreed to this, it means audience also believes that cinema portrays men like ideal and supermen. They do not show how a normal man is in real life which protects and take cares of his family but not behaves like superhero which Indian cinema depicts.

The analysis of the above data shows that Indian cinema is showing the Indian culture in negative way and trying to manipulate the beliefs of the audience and the youth of India which follows Indian cinema.

Gender Quality in Cinema

The responses on the general beliefs shows that women is not on equal foot with men in the society. Now to understand how cinema portrays women, different statements were made in front of them on which they responded on a scale from strongly disagree to strongly agree. Following are the distributions of the responses received from the participants of survey.

Table 5.4: Perceptions towards gender equality in Indian cinema

Statement	Strongly Disagree	Disagree	Neutral	Agree	Strongly agree
Indian cinema depicts women as dependent on men	2.0	9.8	28.1	41.0	19.1
Indian cinema rarely advocate equal footing of all the genders	2.7	14.8	27.3	37.9	17.2
Indian cinema suggest all the genders as educated, professionals and career oriented equally	4.3	19.9	30.1	35.5	10.2
Indian cinema rarely show women in executive position rather show in subordinate position (clerk, PA) in comparison to men.	3.5	19.1	24.6	34.0	18.8
Indian cinema rarely show women as dominant over man	3.1	15.6	23.8	32.0	25.4

The above table shows that 41% of the respondents agree that Indian cinema depicts women as dependent on men, 28.1 % were neutral, 19.1 % were strongly agree ,9.8% were disagree and 2% were strongly disagree to the statement. Which means most of the respondents agree that Indian cinema shows women as dependent on men. 37.9% of the respondents were agree that Indian cinema rarely advocate the equal footing of all the genders, 27.3 % were neutral, 17.2% were strongly agree, 14.8% were disagree and 2.7% were strongly disagree. It shows that most of the respondents believes that Indian cinema rarely supports equality of all genders. 35.5% of the respondents were agree that Indian cinema suggest all the genders as educated, professionals and career oriented equally, 30.1 % were neutral, 10.2% were strongly agree, 19.9% were disagree and 4.3% were strongly disagree. It shows that most of the respondents believes Indian cinema suggest all the genders as educated, professionals and career oriented equally also a huge proportion (almost 1/3rd) was neutral on this so a firm opinion cannot be given. . 34.0% of the respondents were agree that Indian cinema rarely show women in executive position rather show in subordinate position (clerk, PA) in comparison to men., 24.6% were neutral, 18.8% were strongly agree, 19.1% were disagree and 3.5% were strongly disagree. It shows that most of the respondents reflects that Indian cinema rarely show women in executive position rather show in subordinate position (clerk, PA) in comparison to men. 32.0% of the respondents were agree that Indian cinema rarely show women as dominant over man, 23.8% were neutral, 25.4% were strongly agree, 15.6% were disagree and 3.1% were strongly disagree. It shows that most of the respondents reflects that Indian cinema rarely show women as dominant over man.

The analysis of the data shows that Indian cinema do not shows gender equality, it shows women dependent on men and having less potential and successful than men. In Indian movies women is shown less developed and less educated than men. It shows that Indian cinema supporting gender inequality.

Decision maker

Table 5.5: Perceptions about decision making in Indian cinema

Statement	Strongly disagree	Disagree	Neutral	agree	Strongly Agree
Indian cinema rarely suggest women as the decision makers	.8	13.7	28.1	44.5	12.9

In order to understand the gender subordination, it is very important to know if women are shown as independent decision maker. Almost 1/3rd proportion of the respondents were neutral on this. 44.5 were agree to this, only 12.9 % were strongly agree, 13.7% were disagree and .8were strongly disagree. It shows that most of the respondents believes that Indian cinema rarely shows women as independent decision maker.

Body imaging- Women's body as tool of attraction

In different movies it was observed by the researcher that they use women as a tool for attraction in the movies and use women as a decoration item. For examining what do the audience of the cinema thinks about that following statements were made. The frequency distribution will clearly show what people believe about the same.

Table 5.6: Perceptions about body imaging in Indian cinema

Statement	Strongly disagree	Disagree	Neutral	agree	Strongly agree
Indian cinema shows body and body parts of women excessively and unnecessarily.	1.2	5.1	14.8	27.3	51.6
Indian cinema often show women as 'sex objects'	3.5	7.0	19.1	28.9	41.4
Indian cinema depict young and beautiful actresses.	1.6	4.3	14.5	35.9	43.8
Sometimes I feel uncomfortable while watching movies with my family.	.4	2.3	12.1	34.4	50.8

I would prefer to see actors (normal looking / ordinary) in movies dressed in common fashion rather than extremely beautiful.	1.2	6.3	13.7	35.9	43.0
Indian cinema show women as object of desire.	2.0	9.4	16.0	34.4	38.3

The above table shows that 27.3% of the respondents were agree that Indian cinema shows body and body parts of women excessively and unnecessarily, 14.8% were neutral, 51.6% were strongly agree, 5.1% were disagree and 1.2% were strongly disagree. It shows that most of the respondents reflects that Indian cinema shows body and body parts of women excessively and unnecessarily. 28.9% of the respondents were agree that Indian cinema often show women as 'sex objects', 19.1% were neutral, 41.4% were strongly agree, 7.0% were disagree and 3.5% were strongly disagree. It shows that most of the respondents reflects that Indian cinema often show women as 'sex objects'. 35.9% of the respondents were agree that Indian cinema depict young and beautiful actresses, 14.5% were neutral, 43.8% were strongly agree, 4.3% were disagree and 1.6% were strongly disagree. It shows that most of the respondents reflects that Indian cinema depict young and beautiful actresses. 34.4% of the respondents were agree that sometimes they feel uncomfortable while watching movies with their family, 12.1% were neutral, 50.8% were strongly agree, 2.3% were disagree and .4% were strongly disagree. It shows that most of the respondents reflects that sometimes they feel uncomfortable while watching movies with their family. 35.9% of the respondents were agree that they would prefer to see actors (normal looking / ordinary) in movies dressed in common fashion rather than extremely beautiful, 13.7% were neutral, 43.0% were strongly agree, 6.3% were disagree and 1.2% were strongly disagree. It shows that most of the respondents reflects that they would prefer to see actors (normal looking / ordinary) in movies dressed in common fashion rather than extremely beautiful. 34.4% of the respondents were agree that Indian cinema show women as object of desire, 16% were neutral, 38.3% were strongly agree, 9.4% were disagree and 2.0% were strongly disagree. It shows that most of the respondents reflects that Indian cinema show women as object of desire.

It was always seen that Indian cinema is always dominated by men. The movies are always centred on men in which women are portrayed supporting them or protected by them. In order to know the perception of audience towards patriarchy in Indian cinema following statements were made. The table indicates the distribution of responses recorded-

Table 5.7: Perceptions about patriarchy in Indian cinema

Statement	Strongly disagree	Disagree	Neutral	agree	Strongly agree
Indian cinema often portrays women with their family members and household chores (taking care of the food, health and hygiene of the family)	0.8	7.8	22.3	47.3	21.9
Indian cinema mostly shows women inside the home	4.3	15.2	31.3	33.2	16.0
Indian cinema often shows women in a supporting role for male.	2.7	9.4	14.8	44.1	28.9
Indian cinema often shows that a male is needed to protect her from goons or any situation.	1.2	6.6	12.5	40.2	39.5
Indian cinema is preserving the patriarchy culture.	4.3	7.0	23.4	35.9	29.3

The above table shows that 47.3% of the respondents were agree that Indian cinema often portray women with their family members and household chores (taking care of the food, health and hygiene of the family), 22.3% were neutral, 21.9% were strongly agree, 7.8% were disagree and .8% were strongly disagree. It shows that most of the respondents reflects that Indian cinema often portray women with their family members and household chores (taking care of the food, health and hygiene of the family). 33.2% of the respondents were agree that Indian cinema mostly show women inside the home, 31.3% were neutral, 16.0% were strongly agree, 15.2% were disagree and 4.3% were strongly disagree. It shows that most of the respondents reflects that Indian cinema mostly show women inside the home. 44.1% of the respondents were agree that Indian cinema often show women in a supporting role for male., 14.8% were neutral, 28.9% were strongly agree, 9.4% were disagree and 2.7% were strongly disagree. It shows that most of the respondents reflects that Indian cinema often show women in a supporting role for male. 40.2% of the respondents were agree that Indian cinema often shows that a male is needed to protect her from goons or any situation., 12.5% were neutral, 35.9% were strongly agree, 6.6% were disagree and 1.2% were strongly disagree. It shows that most of the respondents reflects that Indian cinema often shows that a male is needed to protect her from goons or any situation.

35.9% of the respondents were agree that Indian cinema is preserving the patriarchy culture., 23.4% were neutral, 29.3% were strongly agree, 7% were disagree and 4.3% were strongly disagree. It shows that most of the respondents reflects that Indian cinema is preserving the patriarchy culture.

The frequency distributions and analysis indicates that Indian cinema is highly prompting and preserving patriarchy.

Indian cinema has a long history, and change is present everywhere. Cinema also has changed a lot with time. The change comes in many ways like technology, use of places, style of actors, songs and most important the concept of movies. As our concern is with gender subordination so the respondents were asked about the change, they have experience in movies for gender subordination. The following table represents the perception of audience towards the change in cinema.

Table 5.8: Perceptions about revolution in Indian cinema

Statement	**Strongly disagree**	**Disagree**	**Neutral**	**Agree**	**Strongly agree**
Indian cinema has evolved in terms of gender Subordination	3.1	8.2	27.0	43.8	18.0
Indian cinema portrays the condition of the society in realistic way.	9.4	16.8	29.7	32.0	12.1

The above table shows that 43.8% of the respondents were agree that Indian cinema has evolved in terms of gender subordination, 27% were neutral, 18.0% were strongly agree, 8.2% were disagree and 3.1% were strongly disagree. It shows that most of the respondents reflects that Indian cinema has evolved in terms of gender subordination. 32.0% of the respondents were agree that Indian cinema portrays the condition of the society in realistic way, 29.7% were neutral, 12.1% were strongly agree,16.8% were disagree and 9.4% were strongly disagree. It shows that most of the respondents reflects that Indian cinema portrays the condition of the society in realistic way.

India is country of multiplicity and so its cinema is. India almost every state has their own cinema world named on their state or environment which is also called regional cinema. To understand if there are some differences in cinema of different states in terms of culture and gender equality some questions were raised to audience. Following tables represents the results

Table 5.9: Perceptions about differences in regional Cinema

Do you think there is difference in the Cinema of different states (for e.g. Tollywood, Bhojpuri, Pahadiwood, sandalwood, mollywood, Punjabi cinema etc.)?		
	Frequency	Percent
No	19	7.4
Yes	237	92.6
Total	256	100.0

The data shows 92.6% of the respondents believes that there is difference in the Cinema of different states (for e.g. Tollywood, Bhojpuri, Pahadiwood, sandalwood, mollywood, Punjabi cinema etc.). It means that the cinema of different states is different in some ways as they are based on their regional culture and interests.

Table 5.10: Perceptions about portrayal of women in regional cinema

Do you think that the cinema of different states portray women in similar way?		
	Frequency	Percent
No	129	50.4
Yes	127	49.6
Total	256	100.0

The table shows that results are in 50-50 as 50.4% believes that the cinema of different states portray women in different way and 49.6 believes that the cinema of different states portray women in similar way.

Table 5.11: Perceptions about patriarchy in regional cinema

Do you think cinema of all states is preserving patriarchy in their movies?		
	Frequency	Percent
No	87	34.0
Yes	162	66.0
Total	249	100.0

The table shows that the audience believes that cinema of all states is preserving patriarchy in their movies as 66% of them said yes to the question of states cinema preserving patriarchy. It shows that cinema is highly dominating women by men.

Table 5.12: Perceptions about control of government on regional cinema

Do you think that Indian cinema is controlled by State (government)?		
	Frequency	Percent
No	150	58.6
Yes	96	37.5
Total	246	96.1

The responses in the table shows that people do not think that cinema is controlled by governments.

The respondents were asked to give a score out of 5 to indicate how perfectly they portrays the real condition of society through their films.

Table 5.13: Scores for realistic portrayal of society by Indian cinema

Can you please give a score to overall Indian cinema how good they portray the real situation of the society? (1 to 5; 1 means very badly and 5 means perfectly).		
	Frequency	Percent
1	30	11.7

2	56	21.9
3	118	46.1
4	39	15.2
5	11	4.3
Total	254	99.2

The table shows that 46.1% of respondents gave a score of 3, 21.9% gave a score of two, 15.2 percent gave a score of 4, 11.7% gave a score of 1 and 4.3% gave a score of 5. The data shows that most of the responses were recorded up to a score of 3 which means that most of the responses says Indian cinema portrays the situation of society from very badly to average. Most of the responses were recorded for a score of 3 which means that most of the people believe that Indian cinema portrays the condition of society on average level.

When we watch something, it impacts ourselves in some way. This impact could be in any way like thinking, behaviour, our routine etc. As our objective is to understand cinema affects the everyday life of audience. The following table represents the obtained results-

Table 5.14: Perceptions about effect of Indian cinema on everyday life

Indian Cinema influences our everyday life		
	Frequency	Percent
Strongly disagree	8	3.1
Disagree	11	4.3
Neutral	47	18.4
Agree	97	37.9
Strongly agree	87	34.0
Total	250	97.7

The above table indicates that only3.1% respondents strongly disagree, 4.3% disagree,18.4% were neutral,37.9% were agree and 34.0% were strongly agree that cinema influences the everyday life of its audience. The frequency distribution indicates that most of the respondents believes that if affects the everyday life of people.

As our study is aimed towards gender subordination and cultural hegemony, then it becomes very important to analyze the perspective of different genders about the same. We can find out the difference between the thinking process of the males and females about the content of Indian cinema. A statistical analysis will show if that difference between the responses of males and females is significant or not.

Under the variable gender equality 7 items were considered. The items were representing the statements about equality of genders in Indian cinema. In order to understand the belief of different genders about the content shown in the movies about all genders. The following frequency distribution represents the responses of males and females separately.

Table 5.15: Gender wise Perceptions about Indian cinema depicting women as dependent on men

Indian cinema depicts women as dependent on men				
		Gender		Total
		Female	Male	
Indian cinema depicts women as dependent on men	Strongly disagree	1.4%	2.6%	2.0%
	Disagree	8.6%	11.1%	9.8%
	Neutral	29.5%	26.5%	28.1%
	Agree	43.2%	38.5%	41.0%
	Strongly agree	17.3%	21.4%	19.1%
Total		100.0%	100.0%	100.0%

Table 5.16: Gender wise Perceptions about Indian cinema rarely advocating equal footing of all the genders

Indian cinema rarely advocate equal footing of all the genders				
		Gender		**Total**
		Female	**Male**	
Indian cinema rarely advocate equal footing of all the genders	Strongly disagree	3.6%	1.7%	2.7%
	Disagree	11.5%	18.8%	14.8%
	Neutral	25.9%	29.1%	27.3%
	Agree	41.7%	33.3%	37.9%
	Strongly agree	17.3%	17.1%	17.2%
Total		100.0%	100.0%	100.0%

Table 5.17: Gender wise Perceptions about Indian cinema suggesting all the genders as educated, professionals and career oriented equally

Indian cinema suggest all the genders as educated, professionals and career oriented equally				
		Gender		Total
		Female	Male	
Indian cinema suggest all the genders as educated, professionals and career oriented equally	Strongly disagree	6.5%	1.7%	4.3%
	Disagree	16.5%	23.9%	19.9%
	Neutral	28.8%	31.6%	30.1%
	Agree	36.0%	35.0%	35.5%
	Strongly agree	12.2%	7.7%	10.2%
Total		100.0%	100.0%	100.0%

Table 5.18: Gender wise Perceptions about Indian cinema rarely showing women in executive position rather show in subordinate position (clerk, PA) in comparison to men

Indian cinema rarely show women in executive position rather show in subordinate position (clerk, PA) in comparison to men				
		Gender		**Total**
		Female	**Male**	
Indian cinema rarely show women in executive position rather show in subordinate position (clerk, PA) in comparison to men.	Strongly disagree	2.9%	4.3%	3.5%
	Disagree	18.0%	20.5%	19.1%
	Neutral	25.2%	23.9%	24.6%
	Agree	34.5%	33.3%	34.0%
	Strongly agree	19.4%	17.9%	18.8%
Total		100.0%	100.0%	100.0%

Table 5.19: Gender wise Perceptions about Indian cinema rarely showing women as dominant over man men

Indian cinema rarely show women as dominant over man				
		Gender		**Total**
		Female	**Male**	
Indian cinema rarely show women as dominant over man	Strongly disagree	2.2%	4.3%	3.1%
	Disagree	12.9%	18.8%	15.6%
	Neutral	23.7%	23.9%	23.8%

	Agree	33.1%	30.8%	32.0%
	Strongly agree	28.1%	22.2%	25.4%
Total		100.0%	100.0%	100.0%

The above table indicates that 1.4% females were disagree and 2.6% males were disagreeing that Indian cinema depicts women as dependent on men. 8.6% females were disagreeing and 11.1% males were disagreeing, 29.5% males were neutral and 26.5 % males were neutral, 43.2% females were agreeing to this and 38.5 males were agreeing, 17.3% females were strongly agreeing and 21.4% males were strongly agreeing.

On total 60.5% females were agreeing and 59.9% males were agreeing, it shows that almost equal number of males and females feels that Indian cinema depicts women as dependent on men.

The above table indicates that 3.6% females were disagree and 1.7% males were disagree that Indian cinema rarely advocate equal footing of all the genders.11.5% females were disagree and 18.8% males were disagree, 25.9% females were neutral and 29.1% males were neutral, 41.7% females were agree to this while only 33.3% males were agree, 17.3% females were strongly agree and 17.1% males were strongly agree.

On total 69.0% females were agreeing and 50.4% males were agreeing, it shows that a smaller number of males feels that Indian cinema rarely advocate equal footing of all the genders in comparison to women.

The above table indicates that 6.5% females were disagree and 1.7% males were disagree that Indian cinema suggest all the genders as educated, professionals and career oriented equally.16.5% females were disagree and 23.9 % males were disagree, 28.8% females were neutral and 31.6% males were neutral, 36.0% females were agree to this while only 35.0% males were agree, 12.2% females were strongly agree and 7.7% males were strongly agree.

On total 48.2% females were agreeing and 42.7% males were agreeing, it shows that a smaller number of males feels Indian cinema suggest all the genders as educated, professionals and career oriented equally in comparison to women.

The above table indicates that 2.9% females were disagree and 4.3% males were disagreeing that Indian cinema rarely show women in executive position rather show in subordinate position (clerk, PA) in comparison to men. 18.0% females were disagreeing and 20.5% males were disagreeing, 25.2% females were neutral and 23.9% males were neutral, 34.5% females were agreeing to this while only 33.3% males were agreeing, 19.4% females were strongly agreeing and 17.9% males were strongly agreeing.

On total 53.9% females were agreeing and 51.2% males were agreeing, it shows that a smaller number of males feels Indian cinema rarely show women in executive position rather show in subordinate position (clerk, PA) in comparison to men.

The above table indicates that 2.2% females were disagree and 4.3% males were strongly disagreeing that Indian cinema rarely show women as dominant over man. 12.9% females were disagreeing and 18.8% males were disagreeing, 23.7% females were neutral and 23.9% males were neutral, 33.1% females were agreeing to this while only 23.9% males were agreeing, 33.1% females were strongly agreeing and 30.8% males were strongly agreeing.

On total 61.2% females were agreeing and 53.0% males were agreeing, it shows that a smaller number of males feels Indian cinema rarely show women as dominant over man.

The respondents were asked according to them who is shown taking decision in Indian cinema. The following table represents the gender wise distribution of the responses.

Table 5.20: Gender wise Perceptions about decision making in Indian cinema

Indian cinema rarely suggest women as the decision makers				
		Gender		**Total**
		Female	**Male**	
Indian cinema rarely suggest women as the decision makers	Strongly disagree	1.4%		0.8%
	Disagree	8.6%	19.7%	13.7%
	Neutral	30.2%	25.6%	28.1%
	Agree	45.3%	43.6%	44.5%
	Strongly agree	14.4%	11.1%	12.9%
Total		100.0%	100.0%	100.0%

The above table indicates that 1.4% females were disagree and 0% males were strongly disagreeing that Indian cinema rarely suggest women as the decision makers. 8.6% females were disagreeing and 19.7% males were disagreeing, 30.2% females were neutral and 25.6% males were neutral, 45.3% females were agreeing to this while only 43.6% males were agreeing, 14.4% females were strongly agreeing and 11.1% males were strongly agreeing.

On total 59.7% females were agreeing and 54.7% males were agreeing, it shows that a smaller number of males feels Indian cinema rarely suggest women as the decision makers.

Under the variable body imaging 6 items were considered. The items were representing the statements about body showing in Indian cinema. In order to understand the belief of different genders about the content shown in the movies about excessive use of women's body as a tool of attraction. The following frequency distribution represents the responses of males and females separately.

Table 5.21: Gender wise Perceptions about Indian cinema showing body and body parts of women excessively and unnecessarily

Indian cinema shows body and body parts of women excessively and unnecessarily				
		Gender		Total
		Female	Male	
Indian cinema shows body and body parts of women excessively and unnecessarily	Strongly disagree	2.2%	0	1.2%
	Disagree	3.6%	6.8%	5.1%
	Neutral	11.5%	18.8%	14.8%
	Agree	25.9%	29.1%	27.3%
	Strongly agree	56.8%	45.3%	51.6%
Total		100.0%	100.0%	100.0%

The above table indicates that 2.2% females were disagree and 0% males were disagreeing that Indian cinema shows body and body parts of women excessively and unnecessarily. 3.6% females were disagreeing and 6.8% males were disagreeing, 11.5% females were neutral and 18.8% males were neutral, 25.9% females were agreeing to this while only 29.1% males were agreeing, 56.8% females were strongly agreeing and 45.3% males were strongly agreeing.

On total 82.7% females were agreeing and 74.4% males were agreeing, it shows that a smaller number of males feels Indian cinema shows body and body parts of women excessively and unnecessarily. The proportion of participant believing the about the body show of women in movies is huge and shows that almost all believe that they show women body excessively.

Table 5.22: Gender wise Perceptions about Indian cinema often showing women as 'sex objects'.

Indian cinema often show women as 'sex objects'.				
		Gender		Total
		Female	Male	
Indian cinema often show women as 'sex objects'	Strongly disagree	2.2%	5.1%	3.5%
	Disagree	5.0%	9.4%	7.0%
	Neutral	23.0%	14.5%	19.1%
	Agree	26.6%	31.6%	28.9%
	Strongly agree	43.2%	39.3%	41.4%
Total		100.0%	100.0%	100.0%

The above table indicates that 2.2% females were disagree and 5.1% males were strongly disagreeing that Indian cinema often show women as 'sex objects'. 5.0% females were disagreeing and 9.4% males were disagreeing, 23.0% females were neutral and 14.5% males were neutral, 33.1% females were agreeing to this and 31.6% males were agreeing, 43.2% females were strongly agreeing and 39.3% males were strongly agreeing.

On total 69.8% females were agreeing and 70.9% males were agreeing, it shows that almost equal number of males and females feels Indian cinema often show women as 'sex objects'.

Table 5.23: Gender wise Perceptions about Indian cinema depicting young and beautiful actresses.

Indian cinema depict young and beautiful actresses				
		Gender		Total
		Female	Male	
Indian cinema depict young and beautiful actresses	Strongly disagree	0.7%	2.6%	1.6%
	Disagree	4.3%	4.3%	4.3%
	Neutral	18.0%	10.3%	14.5%
	Agree	27.3%	46.2%	35.9%
	Strongly agree	49.6%	36.8%	43.8%
Total		100.0%	100.0%	100.0%

The above table indicates that .7% females were disagree and 2.6% males were strongly disagreeing that Indian cinema depict young and beautiful actresses. 4.3% females were disagreeing and 4.3% males were disagreeing, 18.0% females were neutral and 10.3% males were neutral, 27.3% females were agreeing to this and 46.2% males were agreeing, 49.6% females were strongly agreeing and 36.8% males were strongly agreeing.

On total 76.9% females were agreeing and 82.0% males were agreeing, it shows that a smaller number of females feels Indian cinema depict young and beautiful actresses.

Table 5.24: Gender wise Perceptions about non-comfort in watching cinema with family.

Sometimes I feel uncomfortable while watching movies with my family				
		Gender		Total
		Female	Male	
Sometimes I feel uncomfortable while watching movies with my family	Strongly disagree	0.7%	0	0.4%
	Disagree	2.2%	2.6%	2.3%
	Neutral	9.4%	15.4%	12.1%

	Agree	32.4%	36.8%	34.4%
	Strongly agree	55.4%	45.3%	50.8%
Total		100.0%	100.0%	100.0%

The above table indicates that .7% females were disagreeing and 0% males were strongly disagreeing that sometimes it is uncomfortable while watching movies with family. 2.2% females were disagreeing and 2.6% males were disagreeing, 9.4% females were neutral and 15.4% males were neutral, 32.4% females were agreeing to this and 36.8% males were agreeing, 55.4% females were strongly agreeing and 45.3% males were strongly agreeing.

On total 87.8% females were agreeing and 82.1% males were agreeing, it shows that a smaller number of males feels sometimes it is uncomfortable while watching movies with family.

Table 5.25: Gender wise Perceptions about preference to see actors (normal looking / ordinary) in movies dressed in common fashion rather than extremely beautiful

I would prefer to see actors (normal looking / ordinary) in movies dressed in common fashion rather than extremely beautiful

		Gender		Total
		Female	Male	
I would prefer to see actors (normal looking / ordinary) in movies dressed in common fashion rather than extremely beautiful	Strongly disagree	0.7%	1.7%	1.2%
	Disagree	3.6%	9.4%	6.3%
	Neutral	14.4%	12.8%	13.7%
	Agree	29.5%	43.6%	35.9%
	Strongly agree	51.8%	32.5%	43.0%
Total		100.0%	100.0%	100.0%

The above table indicates that .7% females were disagree and 1.7% males were strongly disagreeing that they would prefer to see actors (normal looking / ordinary) in movies dressed in common fashion rather than extremely beautiful. 3.6% females were disagreeing and 9.4% males were disagreeing, 14.4% females were neutral and 12.8% males were neutral,29.5% females were agreeing to this while only 43.6% males were agreeing, 51.8% females were strongly agreeing and 32.5% males were strongly agreeing.

On total 81.3 % females were agreeing and 76.1% males were agreeing, it shows that a smaller number of males feels that they would prefer to see actors (normal looking / ordinary) in movies dressed in common fashion rather than extremely beautiful.

Table 5.26: Gender wise Perceptions about Indian cinema showing women as object of desire

Indian cinema show women as object of desire				
		Gender		**Total**
		Female	**Male**	
Indian cinema show women as object of desire	Strongly disagree	1.4%	2.6%	2.0%
	Disagree	5.0%	14.5%	9.4%
	Neutral	16.5%	15.4%	16.0%
	Agree	33.1%	35.9%	34.4%
	Strongly agree	43.9%	31.6%	38.3%
Total		100.0%	100.0%	100.0%

The above table indicates that 1.4% females were disagreeing and 2.6% males were strongly disagreeing that Indian cinema show women as object of desire. 5.0% females were disagreeing and 14.5% males were disagreeing, 16.5% females were neutral and 15.4% males were neutral, 33.1% females were agreeing to this while only 35.9% males were agreeing, 43.9% females were strongly agreeing and 31.6% males were strongly agreeing.

On total 77.0 % females were agreeing and 51.3% males were agreeing, it shows that a smaller number of males feel Indian cinema show women as object of desire.

Under the variable patriarchy in cinema 5 items were considered. The items were representing the statements about body showing in Indian cinema. In order to understand the belief of different genders about the content shown in the movies about women being housewife and asking help from men. The following frequency distribution represents the responses of males and females separately.

Table 5.27: Gender wise Perceptions about Indian cinema often portraying women with their family members and household chores.

Indian cinema often portray women with their family members and household chores (taking care of the food, health and hygiene of the family)				
		Gender		**Total**
		Female	**Male**	
Indian cinema often portray women with their family members and household chores (taking care of the food, health and hygiene of the family)	Strongly disagree	0.7%	0.9%	0.8%

	Disagree	5.0%	11.1%	7.8%
	Neutral	23.0%	21.4%	22.3%
	Agree	46.0%	48.7%	47.3%
	Strongly agree	25.2%	17.9%	21.9%
Total		100.0%	100.0%	100.0%

The above table indicates that .7% females were disagree and .9% males were strongly disagreeing that Indian cinema often portray women with their family members and household chores (taking care of the food, health and hygiene of the family). 5.0% females were disagreeing and 11.1% males were disagreeing, 23.0% females were neutral and 21.4% males were neutral, 46.0% females were agreeing to this and 48.7% males were agreeing, 25.2% females were strongly agreeing and 17.9% males were strongly agreeing.

On total 71.2% females were agreeing and 66.6% males were agreeing, it shows that a smaller number of males feels Indian cinema often portray women with their family members and household chores (taking care of the food, health and hygiene of the family).

Table 5.28: Gender wise Perceptions about Indian cinema mostly showing women inside the home

Indian cinema mostly show women inside the home				
		Gender		**Total**
		Female	**Male**	
Indian cinema mostly show women inside the home	Strongly disagree	4.3%	4.3%	4.3%
	Disagree	14.4%	16.2%	15.2%
	Neutral	34.5%	27.4%	31.3%
	Agree	31.7%	35.0%	33.2%
	Strongly agree	15.1%	17.1%	16.0%
Total		100.0%	100.0%	100.0%

The above table indicates that 4.3% females were disagree and 4.3% males were strongly disagreeing that Indian cinema mostly show women inside the home. 14.4% females were disagreeing and 16.2% males were disagreeing, 34.5% females were neutral and 27.4% males were neutral, 31.7% females were agreeing to this and 35.0% males were agreeing, 15.1% females were strongly agreeing and 17.1% males were strongly agreeing.

On total 46.8% females were agreeing and 52.1% males were agreeing, it shows that a smaller number of females feels Indian cinema mostly show women inside the home.

Table 5.29: Gender wise Perceptions about Indian cinema often showing women in a supporting role for male

Indian cinema often show women in a supporting role for male				
		Gender		Total
		Female	Male	
Indian cinema often shows women in a supporting role for male.	Strongly disagree	1.4%	4.3%	2.7%
	Disagree	7.9%	11.1%	9.4%
	Neutral	14.4%	15.4%	14.8%
	Agree	46.8%	41.0%	44.1%
	Strongly agree	29.5%	28.2%	28.9%
Total		100.0%	100.0%	100.0%

The above table indicates that 1.4% females were disagree and 4.3% males were strongly disagreeing Indian cinema often show women in a supporting role for male. 7.9% females were disagreeing and 11.1% males were disagreeing, 14.4% females were neutral and 15.4% males were neutral, 46.8% females were agreeing to this while only 41.0% males were agreeing, 29.5% females were strongly agreeing and 28.2% males were strongly agreeing.

On total 76.3% females were agreeing and 69.2% males were agreeing, it shows that a smaller number of males feels Indian cinema often show women in a supporting role for male.

Table 5.30: *Gender wise Perceptions about Indian cinema often showing that a male is needed to protect her from goons or any situation.*

Indian cinema often shows that a male is needed to protect her from goons or any situation.				
		Gender		Total
		Female	Male	
Indian cinema often shows that a male is needed to protect her from goons or any situation.	Strongly disagree	0.7%	1.7%	1.2%
	Disagree	4.3%	9.4%	6.6%
	Neutral	12.2%	12.8%	12.5%
	Agree	38.8%	41.9%	40.2%
	Strongly agree	43.9%	34.2%	39.5%
Total		100.0%	100.0%	100.0%

The above table indicates that .7% females were disagree and 1.7% males were strongly disagreeing Indian cinema often shows that a male is needed to protect her from goons or any situation. 4.3% females were disagreeing and 9.4% males were disagreeing, 12.2% females were neutral and 12.8% males were neutral, 38.8% females were agreeing to this while only 41.9% males were agreeing, 43.9% females were strongly agreeing and 34.2% males were strongly agreeing.

On total 82.7% females were agreeing and 75.1% males were agreeing, it shows that a smaller number of males feels Indian cinema often shows that a male is needed to protect her from goons or any situation.

Table 5.31: Gender wise Perceptions about Indian cinema preserving the patriarchy culture

Indian cinema is preserving the patriarchy culture.				
		Gender		**Total**
		Female	**Male**	
Indian cinema is preserving the patriarchy culture.	Strongly disagree	3.6%	5.1%	4.3%
	Disagree	5.8%	8.5%	7.0%
	Neutral	23.7%	23.1%	23.4%
	Agree	34.5%	37.6%	35.9%
	Strongly agree	32.4%	25.6%	29.3%
Total		100.0%	100.0%	100.0%

The above table indicates that 3.6% females were disagree and 5.1% males were strongly disagreeing Indian cinema is preserving the patriarchy culture. 5.8% females were disagreeing and 8.5% males were disagreeing, 23.7% females were neutral and 23.1% males were neutral, 34.5% females were agreeing to this while only 37.6% males were agreeing, 32.4% females were strongly agreeing and 25.6% males were strongly agreeing.

On total 66.9% females were agreeing and 63.2% males were agreeing, it shows that a smaller number of males feels Indian cinema is preserving the patriarchy culture.

Under the variable patriarchy in cinema 2 items were considered. The items were representing the statements about change in cinema showing in Indian cinema. In order to understand the belief of different genders about the content shown in the movies about evolution. The following frequency distribution represents the responses of males and females separately.

Table 5.32: Gender wise Perceptions about evolution of Indian cinema in terms of gender subordination

Indian cinema has evolved in terms of gender subordination				
		Gender		**Total**
		Female	**Male**	
Indian cinema has evolved in terms of gender subordination	Strongly disagree	2.9%	3.4%	3.1%
	Disagree	7.2%	9.4%	8.2%
	Neutral	33.8%	18.8%	27.0%
	Agree	41.7%	46.2%	43.8%
	Strongly agree	14.4%	22.2%	18.0%
Total		100.0%	100.0%	100.0%

The above table indicates that 2.9% females were disagree and 3.4% males were strongly disagreeing Indian cinema has evolved in terms of gender subordination. 7.2% females were disagreeing and 9.4% males were disagreeing, 33.8% females were neutral and 18.8 % males were neutral,41.7% females were agreeing to this and 46.2% males were agreeing, 14.4% females were strongly agreeing and 22.2% males were strongly agreeing.

On total 56.1% females were agreeing and 68.4% males were agreeing, it shows that a smaller number of females feels Indian cinema has evolved in terms of gender subordination.

Table 5.33: Gender wise Perceptions about Indian cinema portraying the condition of the society in realistic way.

Indian cinema portrays the condition of the society in realistic way.				
		Gender		**Total**
		Female	**Male**	
Indian cinema portrays the condition of the society in realistic way.	Strongly disagree	12.2%	6.0%	9.4%
	Disagree	18.0%	15.4%	16.8%
	Neutral	36.0%	22.2%	29.7%
	Agree	25.9%	39.3%	32.0%
	Strongly agree	7.9%	17.1%	12.1%
Total		100.0%	100.0%	100.0%

The above table indicates that 12.2% females were disagree and 6.0% males were strongly disagreeing Indian cinema has evolved in terms of gender subordination. 18.0% females were disagreeing and 15.4% males were disagreeing, 36.0% females were neutral and 22.2% males were neutral, 25.9% females were agreeing to this and 39.3% males were agreeing, 7.9% females were strongly agreeing and 17.1% males were strongly agreeing.

On total 33.8% females were agreeing and 56.4% males were agreeing, it shows that a smaller number of females feels Indian cinema has evolved in terms of gender subordination. The data shows that a smaller number of males and females believes that Indian cinema portray the society realistically.

Comparison between the perceptions on the basis of age, gender and marital status

The purpose is to understand the perception of people towards cultural hegemony and gender subordination in Indian cinema. There are many important factors according which the perception may vary like age Gender and marital status. People of different age group may have different opinion, like young and middle-aged people may have different opinion about the content shown in the movies similarly people gender may have significant impact on the thinking process, like men may think that cinema is motivating women while women may think that it is not motivating for them. Marital status may also impact the thinking process as married and unmarried people live in totally different environment. In order to understand whether there is a significant difference between the responses on the basis of age, gender and marital status, Mann-Whitney U and Kruskal- wallis test were employed. Following are the results obtained-

Impact of Gender

Table 5.34: Gender wise Ranks from Mann-Whitney U test

Ranks				
Variable	**Gender**	**N**	**Mean Rank**	**Sum of Ranks**
Gender Equality	Female	139	132.17	18239.00
	Male	117	123.09	14401.00
	Total	256		
Body imaging	Female	139	134.72	18726.00
	Male	117	121.11	14170.00
	Total	256		
Patriarchy	Female	139	138.75	19286.50
	Male	117	116.32	13609.50
	Total	256		

Decision making	Female	139	133.95	18619.50
	Male	117	122.02	14276.50
	Total	256		
Change in cinema				
Indian cinema has evolved in terms of gender subordination	Female	139	121.20	16847.00
	Male	117	137.17	16049.00
	Total	256		
Indian cinema portrays the condition of the society in realistic way.	Female	139	114.61	15930.50
	Male	117	145.00	16965.50
	Total	256		

Table 5.35: Results of Mann-Whitney U test for impact of gender

Variable	Mann-Whitney U	Wilcoxon W	Z	Sig. (2- tailed)
Gender Equality	7498	14401	-1.027	0.304
Body imaging	7267	14170	-1.598	0.11
Patriarchy	6706.5	13609.5	-2.6	0.009
Decision making	7373.5	14276.5	-1.365	0.172
Change in Cinema				
Indian cinema has evolved in terms of gender Subordination	7117.50	16847	-2.822	0.048
Indian cinema portrays the condition of the society in realistic way.	6200.500	15930.500	-3.386	.001

Gender equality: The results of Mann-Whitney U test shows that there is no significant difference between the perception of male and female regarding gender equality as (Z= -1.207 and p =.304>.05). The mean rank for female is 132.17 while for male mean rank is 123.09. An examination of men rank indicates that females have more scores than males in gender equality, as the items were indicating that more females agree that there is no gender equality in cinema. Thus, it is concluded that there is perception about gender equality in Indian cinema do not significantly differs across genders. They both have same perception about the content of cinema about genders.

Body imaging

The results of Mann-Whitney U test shows that there is no significant difference between the perception of male and female regarding body imaging as (Z= -1.5.98

and p =.11>.05). The mean rank for female is 134.72 while for male mean rank is 121.11. An examination of mean rank indicates that females have more scores than males for body imaging perception, as the data shows more women believe that cinema uses women's body excessively and as a tool for attraction. Thus, it is concluded that there is perception about body imaging and body show in Indian cinema do not significantly differs across genders. Both the genders equally believe that cinema shows and uses women body to attract the audience and also use it as sex object.

Patriarchy

The results of Mann-Whitney U test shows that there is a significant difference between the perception of male and female regarding patriarchy as (Z= -2.6 and p =.009<.05). The mean rank for female is 138.75 while for male mean rank is 116.32. An examination of mean rank indicates that females have more scores than males for patriarchy, as the items were indicating that more females agree that there is patriarchy in cinema. Thus, it is concluded that perception about patriarchy in Indian cinema significantly differs across genders. It indicates that more females thinks that there is patriarchy in cinema and less males thinks that there is patriarchy in cinema.

Decision making

The results of Mann-Whitney U test shows that there is no significant difference between the perception of male and female regarding decision making, as (Z= -1.365 and p =.172>.05). The mean rank for female is 133.95 while for male mean rank is 122.02. An examination of mean rank indicates that females have more scores than males for perception about decision making by women, as the data shows more women believe that cinema shows that women do not have right to take decision. Thus, it is concluded that there is perception about decision making by women in Indian cinema do not significantly differs across genders. Both the genders equally believe that cinema rarely show women having equal right to take decision.

Change in cinema

There were only two items in this variable. Mann-Whitney was applied on them separately.

The results of Mann-Whitney U test for first item shows that there is significant difference between the perception of male and female regarding evolution of cinema in terms of gender subordination, as (Z= -2.822 and p =.048<.05). The mean rank for female is 121.95 while for male mean rank is 137.02. An examination of mean rank indicates that males have more scores than females for perception about change in cinema by women, as the data shows more men believe that cinema has evolved in terms of gender subordination. Thus, it is concluded that there is perception about evolution in terms of gender subordination Indian cinema significantly differs across genders. More no of males believes that cinema has evolved than females.

The results of Mann-Whitney U test for second item shows that there is significant difference between the perception of male and female regarding realistic portrayal of society, as (Z= -3.386 and p =.001<.05). The mean rank for female is 114.61 while for male mean rank is 142.2. An examination of mean rank indicates that males have more scores than females for perception about realistic portrayal of society, as the data shows more men believe that cinema always shows the real condition of society. Thus, it is concluded that there is perception about the realistic show of society by Indian cinema significantly differs across genders. More number of males than females believes that cinema has evolved.

Both the items are showing that there is significant difference between the perceptions of males and females about the change in cinema ,it could be believed that perception about change in cinema differs across gender and males more than females believes that change has occurred.

Impact of Age

Table 5.36: Age wise Ranks from Kruskal-Wallis test

Variables	Age Groups	N	Mean Rank
Gender Equality	18-25 years	154	127.85
	25-35 years	64	127.70
	35-45 years	25	121.18
	Above 45 years	12	145.75
	Total	255	
Body imaging	18-25 years	154	129.70
	25-35 years	64	126.79
	35-45 years	26	124.21
	Above 45 years	12	131.46
	Total	256	
Patriarchy	18-25 years	154	130.17
	25-35 years	64	126.85
	35-45 years	26	120.15
	Above 45 years	12	133.92
	Total	256	

Decision Making	18-25 years	154	120.40
	25-35 years	64	137.51
	35-45 years	26	144.90
	Above 45 years	12	148.83
	18-25 years	256	
Change in cinema			
Indian cinema portrays the condition of the society in realistic way.	18-25 years	154	121.60
	25-35 years	64	132.59
	35-45 years	26	151.08
	Above 45 years	12	146.38
	Total	256	
Indian cinema has evolved in terms of gender subordination.	18-25 years	154	129.70
	25-35 years	64	126.79
	35-45 years	26	124.21
	Above 45 years	12	131.46
	Total	256	

Table 5.37: Results of Kruskal-Wallis test for impact of age

Variables	Chi square	Degree of freedom	Sig. (2-tailed)
Gender Equality	1.000	3	.801
Body imaging	.216	3	.975
Patriarchy	.585	3	.900
Decision making	5.582	3	.134
Change in cinema			
Indian cinema has evolved in terms of gender subordination	4.980	3	.173
Indian cinema portrays the condition of the society in realistic way.	4.283	3	.233

Gender equality

The results of Kruskal wallis test shows that there is no significant difference between the perception of different age groups regarding gender equality as (□square = 1.00 and p = .801>.05). The mean rank for age group 18-25 is 127.85, mean rank for age group 25-35 is 127.70, mean rank for age group 35-45 years is 121.18 and for above 45 years mean rank is 145.75. An examination of mean rank indicates that age group of above 45 years has more scores than other age groups for gender equality. Thus, it is concluded that perception about gender equality in Indian cinema do not significantly differs across different age groups. All the age groups have same had same perception about the content of cinema about gender's equality.

Body imaging

There were only two items in this variable. Kruskal- wallis was applied on them separately.

The results of Kruskal wallis test for first item shows that there is no significant difference between the perception of different age groups regarding body imaging as (□2 = .216 and p = .900 >.05). The mean rank for age group 18-25 is 129.70, mean rank for age group 25-35 is 126.79, mean rank for age group 35-45 years is 124.21 and for above 45 years mean rank is 131.46. An examination of mean rank indicates that age group of above 45 years has more scores than other age groups for body imaging. Thus, it is concluded that perception about body imaging in Indian cinema do not significantly differs across different age groups. All the age groups have same had same perception about the content of cinema about body imaging. All the groups equally believe that cinema shows and uses women body to attract the audience and also uses it as sex object.

Patriarchy

The results of Kruskal wallis test shows that there is no significant difference between the perception of different age groups regarding patriarchy as (□2 = .585 and p = .975 >.05). The mean rank for age group 18-25 is 130.17, mean rank for age group 25-35 is 126.85, mean rank for age group 35-45 years is 120.15 and for above 45 years mean rank is 133.92. An examination of mean rank indicates that age group of above 45 years has more scores than other age groups for body imaging. Thus, it is concluded that perception about patriarchy in Indian cinema do not significantly differs across different age groups. All the age groups have same had same perception about the content of cinema about patriarchy. All the groups equally believe that cinema preserves patriarchy.

Decision Making

The results of Kruskal- wallis test shows that there is no significant difference between the perception of different age groups regarding decision making of women as (□2 = 5.582 and p = .134 >.05). The mean rank for age group 18-25 is 120.40, mean rank for age group 25-35 is 137.51, mean rank for age group 35-45 years is 144.90 and for above 45 years mean rank is 148.83. An examination of mean rank indicates that age group of above 45 years has more scores than other age groups for body imaging. Thus, it is concluded that perception about decision making in Indian cinema do not significantly differs across different age groups. All the age groups have same had same perception about the content of cinema about decision making by women. All the groups equally believe that cinema rarely show women having equal right to take decision.

Change in Cinema

There were only two items in this variable. Kruskal- wallis test was applied on them separately.

The results of Kruskal- wallis test for first item shows that there is no significant difference between the perception of different age groups regarding evolution of cinema in terms of gender subordination as (□2 = 4.980 and p = .173 >.05). The mean rank for age group 18-25 is 129.70, mean rank for age group 25-35 years is 126.79, mean rank for age group 35-45 years is 120.15 and for above 45 years mean rank is 133.92. An examination of mean rank indicates that age group of above 45 years has more scores than other age groups for evolution of cinema in terms of gender subordination. Thus, it is concluded that perception about evolution of cinema in terms of gender subordination in Indian cinema do not significantly differs across different age groups. All the age groups have same had same perception about the content of cinema about evolution of cinema in terms of gender subordination. All the groups equally believe that evolution of cinema in terms of gender subordination, The results of Kruskal- wallis test for second item shows that there is no significant difference between the perception of different age groups regarding realistic portrayal of society as (□2 = 4.283and p = .233 >.05). The mean rank for age group 18-25 is 130.17, mean rank for age group 25-35 is 126.85, mean rank for age group 35-45 years is 120.15 and for above 45 years mean rank is 133.92. An examination of mean rank indicates that age group of above 45 years has more scores than other age groups for realistic portrayal of society. Thus, it is concluded that perception about realistic portrayal in Indian cinema do not significantly differs across different age groups. All the age groups have same had same perception about the content of cinema about evolution of cinema in terms of gender subordination. All the groups equally believe that evolution of cinema in terms realistic portrayal of society. Both the items indicated that there is no significant difference among the different age groups regarding change in cinema.

Impact of Marital Status

Table 5.38: Marital status wise Ranks from Mann-Whitney U test

Ranks				
Variables	**Marital Status**	**N**	**Mean Rank**	**Sum of Ranks**
Gender equality	Married	59	128.77	7468.50
	Unmarried	197	127.77	25171.50
	Total	256		
Body imaging	Married	59	125.22	7388.00
	Unmarried	197	129.48	25508.00
	Total	256		
Patriarchy	Married	59	132.16	7797.50
	Unmarried	197	127.40	25098.50
	Total	256		
Decision Making	Married	59	129.60	7646.50
	Unmarried	197	128.17	25249.50
	Total	256		
Change in cinema				
Indian cinema has evolved in terms of gender subordination	Married	59	133.74	7890.50
	Unmarried	197	126.93	25005.50
	Total	256		
Indian cinema portrays the condition of the society in realistic way.	Married	59	130.81	7718.00
	Unmarried	197	127.81	25178.00
	Total	256		

Table 5.39: Results of Mann-Whitney U test for impact of gender

Variable	**Mann-Whitney U**	**Wilcoxon W**	**Z**	**Sig. (2-tailed)**
Gender Equality	5668.5	25171.5	-0.094	0.925
Body imaging	5618	7388	-0.423	0.672
Patriarchy	5595.5	25098.5	-0.466	0.641
Decision making	5746.5	25249.5	-0.139	0.89
Indian cinema has volved in terms of gender subordination	5502.5	25005.5	-0.656	0.512

Indian cinema portrays-the condition of the society in realistic way.	5675	25178	-0.283	0.777

Gender equality

The results of Mann-Whitney U test shows that there is no significant difference between the perception of married and unmarried people regarding gender equality as (Z= -0.094 and p =.925>.05). The mean rank for married is 128.77 while for unmarried mean rank is 127.77. An examination of men rank indicates that married people have more scores than unmarried people for perception about gender equality. Thus, it is concluded that perception about gender equality in Indian cinema do not significantly differs across marital status. They both have same perception about the content of cinema about genders.

Body imaging

The results of Mann-Whitney U test shows that there is no significant difference between the perception of married and unmarried people body imaging as (Z= -.423 and p =.672>.05). The mean rank for married is 125.22 while for unmarried mean rank is 129.48. An examination of mean rank indicates that unmarried have more scores than married people for body imaging perception. Thus, it is concluded that there is perception about body imaging and body show in Indian cinema do not significantly differs across marital status. Both the categories equally believe that cinema shows and uses women body to attract the audience and also use it as sex object.

Patriarchy

The results of Mann-Whitney U test shows that there is no significant difference between the perception of married and unmarried people regarding patriarchy as (Z= -.466 and p =.641<.05). The mean rank for married is 132.16 while for unmarried mean rank is 127.60. An examination of mean rank indicates that married people have more scores than unmarried people for patriarchy. Thus, it is concluded that perception about patriarchy in Indian cinema do not significantly differs across marital status. It indicates that both the categories equally believe that cinema supports patriarchy.

Decision making

The results of Mann-Whitney U test shows that there is no significant difference between the perception of married and unmarried people regarding decision making, as (Z= -.139 and p =.89 >.05). The mean rank for married is 129.60 while for unmarried mean rank is 128.17. An examination of mean rank indicates that married people have more scores than unmarried people for perception about decision making by women, as the data shows more women believe that cinema shows that women do not have right to take decision. Thus, it is concluded that perception about decision making by women in Indian cinema do not significantly differs across marital status. Both the categories equally believe that cinema rarely show women having equal right to take decision.

Change in cinema

There were only two items in this variable. Mann-Whitney was applied on them separately.

The results of Mann-Whitney U test for first item shows that there is no significant difference between the perception of married and unmarried people regarding evolution of cinema in terms of gender subordination, as (Z= -.656 and p=.512>.05). The mean rank for married people is 133.74 while for unmarried mean rank is 126.93. An examination of mean rank indicates that married people have more scores than unmarried people for perception about change in cinema, thus it is concluded that perception about evolution in terms of gender subordination of Indian cinema do not significantly differs across marital status. Both the categories have same perceptions

The results of Mann-Whitney U test for second item shows that there is no significant difference between the perception of male and female regarding realistic portrayal of society, as (Z= -3.386 and p =.001>.05). The mean rank for married people is 130.81 while for unmarried people mean rank is 127.81. An examination of mean rank indicates that married people have more scores than unmarried people for perception about realistic portrayal of society. Thus, it is concluded that perception about the realistic show of society by Indian cinema do not significantly differs across marital status. Both the items are showing that there is significant difference between the perceptions of males and females about the change in cinema ,it could be believed that perception about change in cinema differs across gender and males more than females believes that change has occurred.

Discussion

The overall results obtained from the primary data shows that both the Indian culture and Indian cinema supports gender subordination. In both the cases women is subordinated and dominated by men. Women is believed to be weak and needed for men's support to survive. Indian cinema uses women as a decorative thing to attract women by showing their body excessively. It very rarely happens that women have a strong role to play in movies. The cinema is now evolving by making some women centered movies but majority is supporting cultural hegemony and gender subordination.

The gender wise distribution of data about beliefs for Indian cinema indicated that there is a variation in responses according gender. The proportions of males and females are different about all the variables. It was found that for larger proportion of females in comparison to males feel that there in gender inequality in cinema, cinema is using women as a tool of attraction by showing their body parts, cinema is preserving patriarchy and women do not have equal right to take decision.

The comparative study of these variables on the basis of gender, age and marital status indicated that marital status and age do not have any significant impact on the perception of people towards the cultural hegemony and gender subordination in Indian cinema.

There is a significant impact of gender was found on patriarchy and change in cinema which indicated that the perception of males and females significantly differs for patriarchy and change in cinema.

Chapter 6
Conclusion: Interrogating The Gender Equality Within The Cinemas

A study is presented in research in which the audience of Indian cinema engaged willingly and explored what the opinions of Indian cinema audience on the replication of cultural hegemony and gender subordination. The inference is based on evidence collection from Indian cinema audiences. In keeping with the intent of the analysis a standardized questionnaire was prepared. The survey was circulated via interactive channels such as mail, Whatsapp, etc. with participants. They completed it without any external biases through their own thought mechanism. The survey form was completed by a total of 256 participants. The study concludes the finding of respondents' thought regarding patterns of Indian culture or cinema and gender subordination in Indian cinema. The frequency distributions of the Reponses demonstrate how the Indian audience feels about the influence of daily cinema and its effects on people's cultural beliefs. It is really interesting to know what people are saying in their own culture and what they think about the subordination of gender in their society before concentrating on cinema. It must be analyzed how gender is viewed in society to see if Indian film content is an actual image of what is happening in society, or whether it is the focus of Indian cinema that drives gender subordination.

They were asked whether the treatment of all genders in society is equivalent, most of the respondents answered that not everybody in society is viewed in equal terms. This indicates that an overwhelming percentage of people assume not both sexes deserve fair care. When asked whether the women of the Indian society are dominated by men, most replied yes, suggesting that in our society women are strongly dominated by men. A question was posed to the respondents as to whether women had the same right and opportunity to take decision. Most respondents replied that women do not have an equal right to make choices in society. In addition, 45.4 percent respondents said yes and 54.6 percent respondents said no, when asked the question, women had the same right to education. So, of 256 respondents almost one half thought women had the same right to education and to choose their profession, and more than one half thought that women do not have rights to make decisions. It indicated that they could not take decisions. There are many goddesses who are believed to be a source of energy and power in Indian society, worshipped as goddess for long time. The respondents were asked whether the treatment of women on the ground indicates that most of the respondents do not even believe women have that kind of respect in Indian society. It means people worship goddess, but real women are considered to be frail. Most respondents concluded that regardless of how well educated or popular a woman is in her profession; she was still obligated to look after her home and her children.

Analysis of people's views of gender equal opportunities and culture reveals that not all sexes in Indian society are viewed equally. Women are governed by men and are supposed to be poorer, dependent on men, and have no choice.

is affecting the cultural beliefs and affecting the mindsets of people about their culture. In order to know what is the perception of the audience of Indian cinema on the point some questions were asked to them about the effects of the movies.

The people were questioned whether Indian cinema attempts to prove that foreign culture is far superior to Indian culture, most of them claim that the cinema displays foreign culture while degrading the Indian culture. A large percentage of people who claim the movies really operate in this way from the point of view of the viewer. The respondents were asked if Indian cinema represents a negative form of Indian culture, most of whom have confidence in it. This means that most people believe that Indian cinema gives us a negative view of the Indian society. The respondents were asked if Indian cinema was attempting to exploit people's cultural values, particularly the young people. It reveals that Indian movies are simply misleading the youth by comparing various faiths and cultures with their cultural values. Following this question, the majority of the respondents agreed if the cinema portrays men over strong, such as battling with many individuals, it indicates the audience still agrees that the movies represent men like values and supermen. They don't demonstrate how average men defend and take care of their families in real life, but they don't mind a superhero portrayed in Indian cinema.

The study from the gathered data suggests that the Indian cinema illustrates Indian culture and manipulates the values of the viewer and the young people in India following Indian cinema in a derogatory way. The answers on general convictions suggest that women in society are not equal to men. Now to see how movies depict women, numerous comments have been made in front of them about the scale of which they firmly agree or disagree.

Most respondents believe that Indian films show women as men's dependents. This means that most people believe that Indian cinema portrays women as men-dependent. The majority of respondents agreed that Indian cinema scarcely supports gender equality. It indicates that most people consider that Indian cinema hardly promotes gender equality. The majority of respondents agreed that Indian films are similarly informed and professional in both genders, with some of them being neutral. This indicates that most respondents agree that Indian film implies that both sexes, as well as educated, professionals and occupations, are equally highly impartial and thus cannot articulate a strong opinion. Most respondents accepted that Indian films seldom depict female executives rather than female subordinates (secretaries, PA) than male. Others were neutral. It indicates that most respondents understand that Indian cinema seldom shows women in the management role as opposed to men (clerk, PA). Most of the respondents concur that Indian films hardly demonstrate that women rule over men. It shows that most respondents agree the Indian cinema's uncommon presence of women over men. The data analyses show that Indian film demonstrates little equality between women and men, showing women that are dependent on men and that they have less potential and more competitive than men. Women are less advanced and less educated than men in Indian films. It reveals that Indian films endorse discrimination between men and women.

It is really interesting to know if women are seen to be autonomous decision makers to consider the subordination of gender. Nearly 1/3 of the respondents have become neutral. Most of them agreed and a few were opposed to this. Most respondents conclude that Indian cinema hardly demonstrates women as autonomous decision-makers. In multiple films, the researcher noticed that women are used in movies as an enticing weapon and that women are used as a decor. And look at what the movie crowd thinks of the following statements.

Most participants accepted that Indian cinema exhibits repetitive, inappropriate and very unfair body and body parts of women. It reveals that most respondents reveal that Indian film exaggerates and excessively reveals anatomy and body parts of women. Most respondents clearly accept that Indian movies frequently show women as 'sex objects' and a few disagree with them. It indicates that most respondents show that Indian cinema often shows women as "sex objects." Many respondents accepted that young and attractive actors are represented in Indian cinema, many accepted and a few disagreed. It reveals that most respondents show that Indian cinema depicts young and lovely actresses. Any respondents admit that when they watch movies with their friends, they often feel awkward, most of them fully agree and very few disagree. It indicates that most respondents reflect that when watching films with their families they often felt awkward. Most respondents believe that in films dressed in common rather than exceptionally glamorous fashion, they would rather see actors (normal looking / normal), of them most firmly agree and few disagree. It indicates that most respondents would like to see actors (normal / ordinary) in common fashion films rather than glamorous ones. Many respondents accepted that Indian cinema was an object of lust for women, many firmly approved and very few disagreed. It shows that most respondents represent Indian cinema's demand for women.

Indian cinema has always been seen to be run by men. The films often concentrate on men who depict people who help or defend them. Most viewers in Indian films accept that women with family members and household duties (with cooking, health and hygiene care) are often depicted in Indian cinema; some viewers were neutral, and very few disagreed. It indicates that the majority of those polled are representing the fact that Indian cinema mostly depicts women with family members and jobs (family care, fitness and hygiene). Most people believe that Indian cinema depicts women mainly within the house, some are neutral and some oppose. It reveals that most of the respondents show that Indian cinema reveals women in the house. Most respondents acknowledged that Indian cinema mostly shows women in male help and few disagree. It indicates that most respondents represent Indian cinema, which also sees women in a position that benefits men. Most respondents believe that Indian film also illustrates that a male is important to shield him from gangs or other circumstance. It shows that most people are reflecting the fact that Indian cinema always shows a man wants to defend her from goons and any circumstances.

The majority of the respondents concur that Indian films maintain the tradition of hegemony and a few disagree strongly. It demonstrates that most people mirror the preservation of patriarchy culture in Indian cinema. Frequency distributions and analysis show that Indian cinema is extremely inspiring and patriarchal.

The history of Indian cinema is long, and progress happens everywhere. Over time too, cinema has changed a lot. Shift happens in several forms such as electronics, location use, acting design and the idea of films. Provided that we are worried with gender subordination, we asked the respondents about the shift that they had in gender subordination films. The table below shows the audience's understanding of cinema transition. Most people believe that Indian cinema has grown in gender subordination, others are neutral, and although very few people disagree strongly. It shows that most respondents represent the evolution of Indian film of gender subordination. Most participants accepted that Indian cinema realistically reflects society's situation and a few disagree. It shows that most respondents represent Indian cinema's objective portrayal of the status of society.

India is a land of variety and its cinema is thus. Nearly every nation has its own film world called regional cinema, or its state or setting. Any questions were put to the audience to clarify why there are such gaps in cinema in various states in terms of culture and sexual freedom. Many of them assume that the cinema of various states varies (e.g. Tollywood, Bhojpuri, Pahadiwood, sandalwood, mollywood, Punjabi film, etc.). In other words, the films of various states are very different as they are based on their popular society and desires.

Half of the people claim that different states' cinemas view women in a different way, and the other half assume that different states' cinemas depict women in a similar manner. The audience assumes that the cinema of all states maintains the patriarchy in their films, as many people agree that the state cinema maintains patriarchy. It reveals that movies are dominated extremely by men.

When we watch something, it impacts ourselves in some way. This impact could be in any way like thinking, behaviour, our routine etc. As our objective is to understand if cinema affects the everyday life of audience. Very few people disagree that cinema influences the everyday life of its audience. The frequency distribution indicates that most of the respondents believe that if affects the everyday life of people.

As our research focuses on subordination of gender and cultural hegemony, discussing gender viewpoints on the same topic becomes very important. We can see the disparity between the male and female thoughts about Indian film content. There has been a comparative study demonstrating whether or not the disparity in male and female responses is important.

Seven things were taken into consideration under the variable gender representation. The essays were comments on gender representation in Indian cinema. to consider the confidence of multiple sexes in the contents of both genders in films. Most women and men accept that Indian film portrays women as dependent on men, and few disagree. Most women agree and most men agree that it illustrates that nearly the same number of men and women think Indian movies show women as men based. Many women disagree with the idea that Indian cinema seldom supports gender equality. Analysis reveals that fewer men believe Indian movies hardly promote equity between both sexes and women.

The study reveals that few females and few males do not believe that Indian film implies that all genders have gender schooling, professions and professions that are similarly geared towards women. Women in executive office seldom reveal a smaller number of men and women in Indian cinema than they do in the subaltern (clerk, PA). Women and men have the impression of Indian cinema being dominated by males.

Many women and men accept that Indian cinema seldom shows that women are decision makers in fewer numbers. Six objects were considered under the variable body imaging. The essays were declarations regarding the body of Indian film. The assumption of multiple genders on the quality of the films on the inappropriate use of women's bodies as an enticing weapon is explored in order to explain. Research reveals that the majority of men and women are agreed that Indian films depict excessive and unnecessary body and body sections of women. The share of participants who believe in women in films is high, suggesting that almost everyone feels they are overly suggesting women.

Both women and men accept that Indian cinema frequently finds women to be 'sex objects' nearly equal to that of men and women. The young and attractive actresses are mainly felt by females and males in Indian film. Both men and women still find that when they watch family movies sometimes it is awkward. Both women and men feel they want to see actors in movies that are popular rather than incredibly attractive (normal / ordinary). Every male and female senses Indian cinema as an object of lust for women.

In cinema, 5 things were considered under the vector patriarchy. The essays were declarations regarding the body of Indian film. To consider the assumption of multiple genders on the contents in the films that women are housewives and ask the help of men. Both men and women accept that Indian films mostly show women with family members and household tasks (friendly cooking, fitness and hygiene).

Most men and women believe that Indian cinema is mainly home for women. Most males and most females accept that Indian films mostly depict women in a position that benefits males. Most people of both genders believe that Indian cinema is always shown to shield a male from goons or something. Most men and women believe that the system of hegemony is preserved in Indian film. 2 elements were regarded under the variable hegemony in film. The items showed the statements on cinema transition in Indian film. To consider the views of separate sexes about the content of evolution seen in the films. Most men and most women accept that Indian films have changed with the subordination of gender. In terms of subordination of sex, most males accept that Indian cinema has advanced. However, most women disagree. The data reveal that less men and women perceive Indian films to be a fair portrayal of society.

We want to consider the view of people in Indian cinema regarding cultural hegemony and female subordination. The interpretation can vary from age to gender and marital status, according to several important factors. People of different age classes may have different opinions. For example, young people and middle-aged people may have different views about the content seen in films; such as men may think that cinema motivates women, whereas women may think that it doesn't inspire them. Marital status may also change the mechanism of reasoning as married and single people live in entirely separate circumstances. To recognize that the reactions on the basis of age, ethnicity and marital status are substantially important.

The findings of the Mann-Whitney-U test show that the view of men and women as a gender equality does not vary significantly. The analysis of the rank of men reveals that women have more points in gender equality than men, as the things have shown that more women believe that cinema does not achieve gender equality. It is also concluded that there is no substantial distinction between gender in Indian cinema. Both of them share the same understanding of the quality of gender cinema.

There is no big difference in the interpretation of men and women in terms of body imagery as a consequence of the Mann-Whitney U test findings. A median grade analysis indicates that women are more likely than men to interpret body imagery, as more women feel that films overuse females' bodies as an attraction weapon. It is also inferred that there is no substantially different understanding of body imagery and body display in Indian cinema. Both men and women agree the film displays and uses women's bodies to lure and even use them as an object of sex.

The findings of the Mann-Whitney-U test indicate that the interpretation of masculine and feminine in relation to patriarchy is substantially different. An analysis of the average rate shows that women earn higher ratings than men, because more women believe that sexism persists in cinema. It has also been concluded that patriarchy expectations vary widely between genders in Indian films. It claims that more women think sexism persists in cinema, and less men think sexism persists in film.

There is no substantial change in the understanding of men and women as regards decision-making based on the outcome of the Mann-Whitney U test. A medium-rank research found that women had more rates than men for their view of women's decision-making, as results showed that more women consider that movies suggest women are not allowed to make decisions. Thus, it is inferred that there is no substantial difference in gender beliefs of decision-making by women in Indian cinema. Both sexes agree fairly the film barely shows women's equal rights to decide.

In terms of gender subordination there is a drastic shift in the understanding of men and women about the evolution of film. A study of the middle range suggests that men experience improvements in cinema by women more than women do, provided that the evidence reveals that more men agree that cinema has changed with respect to the subordination of gender. Thus, it is inferred that there is a major gap between genres in understanding of evolution of the subordination of gender in Indian cinema. There are more men than women who claim that the movies have changed.

The view of men and women on the objective depiction of society varies greatly. A mean rank analysis reveals that males have a higher impression rating than females regarding the actual depiction of society, since the evidence shows that more men assume that movies often reflect the true situation of society. So, it is inferred that there is major difference in gender understanding about the realistic representation of society in Indian film. More men than women think cinema has grown.

The opinion of women and men about the change in cinema varies considerably from the men to women, and it is believed that perception about change in cinema differs across gender and males more than females believes that change has occurred.

The findings of Kruskal's will test indicate that the interpretation of gender representation in different age ranges is not substantially different. A medium-rank exam reveals that the age group over 45 years has more gender equity points than other age groups. It is also concluded that there is no major gap in the understanding of gender equity in Indian cinema across different ages. Both age groups are equally conscious of the content of films surrounding gender equality.

The findings of the Kruskal wallis test indicate that the experience of different age classes in terms of physical imaging is not substantially different. The age group aged more than 45 years gets more points for body imaging than other age ranges. Thus, the interpretation of body imagery in Indian cinema does not vary significantly across various age groups. The same understanding of the cinema content of body imaging is present in all ages. Both groups also agree that the movies portray and use women's bodies to draw the viewer.

The findings of the Kruskal Wallis test indicate that the views of different age groups surrounding patriarchy do not vary greatly. A medium rank exam reveals that the age group above 45 years has more ratings than other body imaging age groups. Thus, the interpretation of patriarchy in Indian film in various age groups does not differs greatly. Both ages have the same understanding of the quality of oppression videos. All people recognize that cinema preserves patriarchy.

The findings of Kruskal- Wallis test reveal that the experience of various age groups as regards decision-making for women does not vary significantly. A medium rank exam reveals that the age group above 45 years has more ratings than other body imaging age groups. It has therefore been concluded that there is no substantial gap in the interpretation of decisions in Indian cinema between different ages. The same perception persists in all age groups about the content of women's decision-making. Both parties agree equally that women are seldom equally able to make choices in film.

The findings of the Kruskal- Wallis test indicate that the understanding of various age groups about films' development in terms of sex subordination does not vary greatly. A medium grade research reveals that age groups over 45 had more findings in terms of gender subordination than other age groups. Thus, the impression that gender in Indian cinema does not vary drastically from one age group to another regarding the evolution of the film. Every age demographic has the same understanding of the quality of cinema about the production of movies in terms of gender subordination. The evolution of cinema as regards gender dependence is similarly claimed by both classes.

The findings of Kruskal- Wallis second item test indicate that the understanding of various age groups as regards the objective portrait of society does not vary greatly. A medium-rank analysis shows that an aggregate over 45 years has more scores for a realistic reflection of culture than other age ranges. Therefore, the understanding of authentic representation in indigenous cinema does not vary substantially between different age groups. The material of cinema concerning cinema's evolution has similar understanding of female subordination in all age groups. The evolution of film in a practical portrait of society is indeed the vision of both classes. The two things demonstrate that there is no major difference in the change in cinema among the numerous age groups.

It has been concluded that there is no major gap in understanding in marital status regarding gender equality in Indian cinema. Both of them share the same understanding of the quality of gender cinema. It has been concluded that there is no major variation between understanding regarding the body imaging and shows between Indian cinema. Both groups also agree the movies display and use women's bodies as a sex symbol to draw and use the viewer. It is concluded that there are no major variations between the views of patriarchy in the Indian cinema. It reveals that both categories often consider that the film encourages patriarchy. It is concluded that there is no major gap in marital understanding of women's decision-making in Indian cinema. Both categories also agree that women are rarely entitled to take decisions in cinema. The conclusion is that there are no major variations in the beliefs about evolution of gender subordination in Indian cinema. The same perceptions apply in all the categories. The results suggest that Indian cinema does not distinguish greatly between the interpretations of the practical display of society. All the things indicate that there is a substantial gap in men's and women's views of change in cinema.

The findings obtained from the primary data reveal that gender subordination is promoted by Indian culture and Indian film. Women are both subordinate and dominated by men in both cases. Women are considered to be frail and men are necessary for the survival of women. Indian films use women to cater to attract people through excessive presentation of their bodies. Women have an important role to play in films quite rarely. The movies are now changing by producing women's films, but most of them perpetuate cultural hegemony and the subordination of genders. The gender-wise distribution of beliefs data for Indian movies reveals that gender responses differ. The male and female proportions vary from each other. It has been discovered that the cinema is used by women as a weapon of attraction by showing their body parts in a greater number of females compared with males as a way of maintaining patriarchy and women have no equal right to make choices in cinema. The comparative study of these factors on the basis of gender and age as well as marital status found that marital status and age had no major effect in

Indian cinema's views of cultural hegemony. The effects of gender on patriarchy and change in cinema have been important, suggesting that the experience of men and women vary considerably in patriarchy and change in cinema.

Appendix: Questionnaire

Title: Gender, Cinema and Society

I am conducting my study on that topic. For determining the perception of the viewers of Indian cinema this survey is to be done. If you are an audience of Indian cinema then Please fill the following questionnaire to help me in my study.

a.) Demographic profile

1. **Name -**
2. **Age –**
3. **Gender**
   a. Male
   b. Female
4. **Marital status**
   a. Married
   b. Unmarried
5. **Education**
   a. Primary
   b. Secondary
   c. Higher
6. **Income level**
   a. Much lower than average
   b. Lower than average
   c. Average
   d. Higher than average
   e. Much higher than average

b.) General information about Indian culture

1. **Do you think that Indian society all genders are treated equally?**
   a. Yes
   b. No
2. **Do you think that women are dominated by men in Indian Society**

a. Yes

b. No

3. **Do you think that women have equal right to take decision in Indian society?**

    a. Yes

    b. No

4. **Do you think in Indian society women have equal rights of education and to make a career choice (this is not about legal right - it is about social right)?**

    a. Yes

    b. No

5. **Indian culture worships goddess, do you think on ground women has the same level respect?**

    a. Yes

    b. No

6. **Do you think in Indian in spite of being educated women are forced to be more oriented towards taking care of home and children?**

    a. Yes

    b. No

c.) Beliefs about Indian cinema:

1. **Do you think that Indian cinema is working in direction to show that foreign culture is much better than Indian culture?**

    a. Yes

    b. No

2. **Do you think that the Indian cinema gives a negative mark of Indian culture on viewers mind?**

    a. Yes

    b. No

3. **Do you think that Indian cinema is manipulating the cultural beliefs of the audience specially the youth?**

    a. Yes

    b. No

4. **Do you think that Indian cinema shows men having more potential**

than real situation (like fighting with multiple people single handed and defeating them)?

a. Yes

b. No

5. **Please read the statements carefully and tick in a box according to the best of your belief.**

Statement	Strongly agree	Agree	Neutral	Disagree	Strongly disagree
Indian cinema depicts women as dependent on men					
Indian cinema rarely advocate equal footing of all the genders					
Indian cinema suggest all the genders as educated, professionals and career oriented equally					
Indian cinema rarely show women in executive position rather show in subordinate position (clerk, PA) in comparison to men.					
Indian cinema rarely show women as dominant over man					
Indian cinema show women as independent decision makers; contributing positively towards the society					
Indian cinema shows body and body parts of women excessively and unnecessarily					
Indian cinema often show women as 'sex objects'					
Indian cinema often portray women with their family members and household chores (taking care of the food, health and hygiene of the family)					
Indian cinema mostly show women inside the home					
Indian cinema depict young and beautiful actresses					
Indian cinema rarely suggest women as the decision makers					
Sometimes I feel uncomfortable while watching movies with my family					
I would prefer to see actors (normal looking / ordinary) in movies dressed in common fashion rather than extremely beautiful					

Indian cinema show women as object of desire					
Indian cinemas often show women in a supporting role for male.					
Indian cinema often shows that a male is needed to protect her from goons or any situation.					
Indian cinema is preserving the patriarchy culture.					
Indian cinema has evolved in terms of gender subordination					
Indian cinema portrays the condition of the society in realistic way.					

6. **Do you think there is difference in the Cinema of different states (for e.g. Tollywood, Bhojpuri, Pahadiwood, Sandalwood, Mollywoood, Punjabi cinema etc.)?**

   a. Yes

   b. No

7. **Do you think that the cinema of different states portray women in similar way?**

   a. Yes

   b. No

8. **Do you think cinema of all states is preserving patriarchy in their movies?**

   a. Yes

   b. No

9. **Can you please give a score to overall Indian cinema how good they portray the real situation of the society? (1 to 5; 1 means very badly and 5 means perfectly).**

   Score – [ ]

10. **Anything to be added from your side. Please write it down.**

Bibliography

Adhia, N. (2013). The role of ideological change in India's economic liberalization. The Journal of Socio-Economics, 44, 103-11.

Agarwal, R. (2014). Changing Roles of Women in Indian Cinema. Humanities, Arts and Social Sciences Studies (Former Name Silpakorn University Journal Of Social Sciences, Humanities, And Arts), 91-106.

Alsford, M. (2006). Heroes and villains. Baylor University Press.

Anand, M., Women in Television: Depictions And Distortions, Women's Studies & Development Centre, Academic Research Centre, University of Delhi. New Delhi.

Bartky, S. L.(1990), Femininity and Domination: Studies in the Phenomenology of Oppression.

Bali, A. (2014). Female Body in Indian Cinema-a Reflection. LinguaInternational Journal of Linguistics, Literature and Culture, 1(1), 93-107.

Beasley, C. (2005). Gender and Sexuality. London: Sage Publications.

Berger, J. (2003). From ways of seeing. The feminism and visual culture reader, 38.

Benyahia, S. C., & Mortimer, C. (2012). Doing film studies. Routledge.

Bhugra, D. (2013). Mad tales from Bollywood: Portrayal of mental illness in conventional Hindi cinema. Psychology Press.

Bose, M. (2008). Bollywood: A history. Roli Books Private Limited.

Bordwell, D., & Thompson, K. (1990). Film Art. An Introduction, McGrow Hill. Inc., New York, 375-379.

Butler, J., (1990). Gender Trouble: Feminism and the Subversion of Identity. Routledge.

Butalia, U. (1984). Woman in Indian Cinema. Feminist Review, 17(1), 108-110.

Carnoy, M. (1986) The State and Political Theory. Cambridge Univ Press.

Chaudhuri, M. (2001, May). Gender and advertisements: The rhetoric of globalisation. In Women's Studies International Forum (Vol. 24, No. 3-4, pp. 373-385). Pergamon.

Chatterjee, P (1989). The nationalist resolution of the women's question (pp. 233-253). na.

Chafetz, J. S. (1997). Feminist theory and sociology: Underutilized contributions for mainstream theory. Annual review of sociology, 23(1), 97120.

Chatterji, S. A. (1998). Subject cinema, object women: a study of the portrayal of women in Indian cinema. Parumita Publications.

Chakravarty, S. (1993) National Identity in Indian popular cinema, 1947-1987, University of Texas.

Chadha, A. (2014). Political participation of women: a case study in India. OIDA International Journal of Sustainable Development, 7(02), 91-108.

Chomsky, N. (2007). Failed states: The abuse of power and the assault on democracy. Metropolitan Books.

Condra, R. (2014). Sensitizing Gender Parity in Urban India: A Cinematic Revolution. International Journal of Advancements in Research & Technology, 3, 91-100.

Currie, G. (1995). Image and Mind: Film, Philosophy and Cognitive Science. Cambridge University Press.

Datta, S. (2000). Globalisation and representations of women in Indian cinema. Social Scientist, 71-82.

Deshpande, A. (2007). Indian cinema and the bourgeois nation state. Economic and political weekly, 95-103.

Debjani, R. (2014). Cinema in the Age of Digital Revolution. International Journal of Interdisciplinary and Multidisciplinary Studies (IJIMS), 1(4), 107-111.

Desai, J. (2004). Beyond Bollywood: The Cultural Politics of South Asian Diasporic Film. Routledge.

Dines, G. and Humez, J.M. (2003). Gender, Race and Class in Media. London: Sage Publications.

Dickey, S. (2009). Fantasy, realism, and other mixed delights: What have film analysts seen in popular Indian cinema?. Projections, 3(2), 1-19.

Dwyer, R. (2003). Lalit Mohan Joshi (ed), Bollywood: Popular Indian Cinema. Contemporary South Asia-Abingdon-, 12(1), 129-129.

Dwyer, R., & Patel, D. (2002). Cinema India: The visual culture of Hindi film. Rutgers University Press.

Facione, P. A. (2011). Critical thinking: What it is and why it counts. Insight assessment, 2007(1), 1-23.

Foucault, M. (1978). The History of Sexuality: Vol. 1, An Introduction. translated from the French by R. Hurley. Penguin Books, 94-96.

Fraser, N. (1989). Unruly Practices: Power, Discourse and Gender in Contemporary Social Theory. Basil Blackwell Ltd.

Gabler, N. (2000). Life the movie: How entertainment conquered reality. Vintage.

Ganti, T. (2013). Bollywood: a guidebook to popular Hindi cinema. Routledge.

Gehlawat, A. (2010). Reframing Bollywood: Theories of Popular Hindi Cinema. Sage Publications.

Ghosh, T. K. (2013). Bollywood Baddies: Villains, vamps and henchmen in Hindi cinema. Sage Publications India.

Gokulsing, K. M., & Dissanayake, W. (Eds.). (2013). Routledge handbook of Indian cinemas. Routledge.

Gokulsing K. M., and Dissanayake W. (1998). Indian Popular Cinema: A Narrative of Cultural Change. London: Trentham Books Limited.

Gopalan, L. (2002). Cinema of interruptions: Action genres in contemporary Indian cinema. British Film Inst.

Gramsci, Antonio. (1975) History, Philosophy and Culture in the Young Gramscied. by Pedro Cavalcanti and Paul Piccone. Telos Press.

Gupta, S.B. & Gupta, S. (2013). Representation of social issues in cinema with specific reference to Indian cinema: case study of Slumdog Millionaire. The Marketing Review. 13(3), 271-282

Gunter, B. (2002). The quantitative research process. A handbook of media and communication research: Qualitative and quantitative methodologies, 209234.

Haskell, M. (2016). From reverence to rape: The treatment of women in the movies. University of Chicago Press.

Heywood, I., & Sandywell, B. (Eds.). (2017). The handbook of visual culture. Bloomsbury Publishing.

Holland, D., & Leander, K. (2004). Ethnographic studies of positioning and subjectivity: An introduction. Ethos, 32(2), 127-139.

Horkheimer, M., & Adorno, T. W. (1972). Dialectic of Enlightenment: Max Horkheimer and Theodor W. Adorono. New York: Seabury Press.

Jackson S. and Scott S. (2002). Gender: A Sociological Reader. London: Routledge.

Jackson S. and Jacjie J. (1998). Contemporary Feminist Theories. Edinburgh: Edinburgh University Press.

Jain, J., & Rai, S. (Eds.). (2002). Films and feminism: Essays in Indian cinema. Rawat Publications.

Jones, Steven. (2006) Antonio Gramsci. London: Routledge.

Juluri, V (2008). Our violence, their violence. Global Bollywood, 117-30.

Kabir, N. M. (2001). Bollywood: the Indian cinema story. Channel 4 Books.

Kapur, J., & Pendakur, M. (2007). The strange disappearance of Bombay from its own cinema: a case of imperialism or globalization?. Democratic Communique, 21(1), 43-43.

Kandiyoti D. (1996). Gendering the Middle East. London: I.B. Tauris Publishers.

Krippendorff, K. (2004). Reliability in content analysis: Some common misconceptions and recommendations. Human communication research, 30(3), 411-433.

Kusuma, K. S. (2018). Female Body and Male Heroism in South Indian Cinema: A Special Reference to Telugu Cinema. Language in India, 18(6).

Levy, A. (2006). Female Chauvinist Pigs: Women and the Rise of Raunch Culture Pocket Books.

Lovell, T. (2002). Lois McNay, Gender and Agency: Reconfiguring the Subject in Feminist and Social Theory. EUROPEAN JOURNAL OF SOCIAL THEORY, 5(2), 296-301.

Lorber, J. (1994). Paradoxes of Gender. New Haven: Yale University Press.

Madaan, N., Mehta, S., Agrawaal, T. S., Malhotra, V, Aggarwal, A., & Saxena, M. (2017). Analyzing Gender Stereotyping in Bollywood Movies. arXiv preprint arXiv:1710.04117.

Manson, Per (red). (2010). Moderna samhallsteorier. Traditioner, riktningar, teoretiker. 8th edition. Stockholm: Norstedt.

McLellan, D. (2007). Marxism after Marx. Palgrave Macmillan.

McRobbie, A. (2009). The aftermath of feminism: Gender, culture and social change. Sage.

Mehta, R. B., & Pandharipande, R. V (Eds.). (2011). Bollywood and globalization: Indian popular cinema, nation, and diaspora. Anthem Press.

Mishra, V. (2006). The Bollywood Cinema: A Critical Genealogy, Asian Studies Institutes, Victoria University of Wellington.

Miegel, Fredrik & Johansson, Thomas. (2002). Kultursociologi.2ndedition. Lund: Studentlitteratur AB.

Miege, B., & Garnham, N. (1979). The cultural commodity. Media, culture & society, 1(3), 297-311.

Mishra, V. (2002). Bollywood cinema: Temples of desire. Psychology Press.

Mohammad, R. (2007). Phir bhi dil hai Hindustani (Yet the heart remains Indian): Bollywood, the 'homeland'nation-state, and the diaspora. Environment and Planning D: Society and Space, 25(6), 1015-1040.

Mulvey, L. (1975). Narrative cinema and visual pleasure. Visual and Other Pleasures.

Murthy, C.S.H.N D. R. (2011). Social Change through Diffusion of Innovation in Indian Popular Cinema: An Analytical Srtudy of Lage Raho Munna Bhai and Stalin. Asian Cinema, 269-289.

Nandakumar, S. (2011). The Stereotypical Portrayal of Women in Commercial Indian Cinema (Doctoral dissertation).

Nair, B. (2002). Female bodies and the male gaze: Laura Mulvey and Hindi cinema. Films and feminism: Essays in Indian cinema, 52-58.

Nevitt, L. (2013). Theatre and Violence. Macmillan International Higher Education.

Nebenzahl, I. D., & Secunda, E. (1993). Consumers' attitudes toward product placement in movies. International journal of advertising, 12(1), 1-11.

Nihalani, G., & Chatterjee, S. (Eds.). (2003). Encyclopaedia of Hindi Cinema. Popular Prakashan.

O'Donnell, V, & Jowett, G. S. (1992). Propaganda and persuasion (p. 116). Sage.

Patel, S. (2003). Bombay and Mumbai: Identities, politics, and populism. Bombay and Mumbai: The city in transition, 3-30.

Prabhu, M. (2001). Roles: reel and real: image of woman in Hindi cinema. Ajanta.

Persson, P. (2003). Understanding cinema: A psychological theory of moving imagery. Cambridge University Press.

Pendakur, M. (2003). Indian popular cinema: Industry, ideology, and consciousness. Hampton Press.

Pillania, R.K. (2008). The Globalization of Indian Hindi Movie Industry. Management Development Institute, India. 3(2), 117.

Prasad, M. M. (2000). Ideology of the Hindi film: A historical construction. Oxford University Press, USA.

Punathambekar, A. (2005). Bollywood in the Indian-American diaspora: Mediating a transitive logic of cultural citizenship. International Journal of Cultural Studies, 8(2), 151-173.

Rasheed, Z., Sheikh, Y, & Shah, M. (2005). On the use of computable features for film classification. IEEE Transactions on Circuits and Systems for Video Technology, 15(1), 52-64.

Rajadhyaksha, A., & Willemen, P. (Eds.). (2014). Encyclopedia of Indian cinema. Routledge.

Ramkissoon, N. (2009). Representations of women in Bollywood cinema: characterisation, songs, dance and dress in Yash Raj films from 1997 to 2007 (Doctoral dissertation).

Ramasubramanian, S., & Oliver, M. B. (2003). Portrayals of sexual violence in popular Hindi films, 1997-99. Sex roles, 48(7-8), 327-336.

Ravi, B. K. (2014). Metamorphosis of Content in Indian Cinema: A Critical Analysis. Educational Research International, 3(3), 65-79.

Ray, S. (1981). Satyajit Ray: An Anthology of Statements on Ray and by Ray. Directorate of Film Festivals, Ministry of Information and Broadcasting, Government of India.

Reinharz, S., & Davidman, L. (1992). Feminist methods in social research. Oxford University Press.

Rishi, T. (2012). Bless You Bollywood!: A Tribute to Hindi Cinema on Completing 100 Years. Trafford Publishing.

Rao, S. (2007). The globalization of Bollywood: An ethnography of non-elite audiences in India. The Communication Review, 10(1), 57-76.

Roy, S. S. (2012). Portrayal Of Women In Indian Media In The Era Of NeoLiberal Economy. Global Media Journal: Indian Edition, 3(1).

Roberge, G. (1990). The subject of Cinema. South Asia Books.

Saunders, M., Lewis, P H. I. L. I. P., & Thornhill, A. D. R. I. A. N. (2007). Research methods. Business Students 4th edition Pearson Education Limited, England.

Shoemaker, P J., & Reese, S. D. (1996). Mediating the message (pp. 781795). White Plains, NY: Longman.

Smith, S. L., & Donnerstein, E. (1998). Harmful effects of exposure to media violence: Learning of aggression, emotional desensitization, and fear. In Human aggression (pp. 167-202). Academic Press.

Sommya, B., Jigna, K., & Madangarli, S. (2012). Mother Maiden Mistress: Women in Hindi Cinema, 1950-2010. Harper Collins.

Srinivas, L. (2002). The active audience: spectatorship, social relations and the experience of cinema in India. Media, Culture & Society, 24(2), 155-173.

Sridhar, S. N., & Mattoo, N. K. (Eds.). (1997). Ananya: A portrait of India. Assn of Indians in Amer.

Stephanie, G., & Benjamin, A. B. (2009). Postfeminism: cultural texts and theories.

Sundar, P (2007). Sounding the nation: The musical imagination of Bollywood cinema (Doctoral dissertation).

Therwath, I. (2010). 'Shining Indians': Diaspora and Exemplarity in Bollywood. South Asia Multidisciplinary Academic Journal, (4).

Tere, N. S. (2012). Gender Reflections in Mainstream Hindi Cinema. Global Media Journal: Indian Edition, 3(1).

UKEssays. November 2018. Representation Of Women In Hindi Cinema Film Studies Essay.

Vasudevan, R. (1996). Shifting codes, dissolving identities: The Hindi social film of the 1950s as popular culture. Third Text, 10(34), 59-77.

Van Zoonen, E. A., & van Zoonen, L. (1994). Feminist media studies (Vol. 9). Sage.

Verma, K. (2019). City and Indian Cinema. Shodhshauryam, International Scientific Refereed Research Journal., 2(1), 173-178.

Virdi, J. (2003). The cinematic imagiNation [sic]: Indian popular films as social history. Rutgers University Press.

Wharton, A. S. (2009). The sociology of gender: An introduction to theory and research. John Wiley & Sons.

Willemen, P., & Rajadhyaksha, A. (1999). Encyclopaedia of Indian cinema.

Index

9 789360 095734

Printed at Repro India Ltd.